Kath Jones was born in 1947 in Eccles, Manchester, where she spent her early childhood. After a Grammar School education in North Wales she started a degree course in mathematics at Oxford, but dropped out after two years to get married. She has been a computer analyst since 1974, when her husband stayed at home to look after the children.

She has since lived in Aberdeen and Mid-Wales and has recently moved to Ayrshire. She has two grown-up children and four grandchildren.

KEEP RIGHT ON TO
THE END OF THE ROAD

Kath Jones

Keep Right On To The End Of The Road

Vanguard Press

A CIP catalogue record for this title is
available from the British Library

ISBN-13: 978 184386 2857
ISBN-10: 1 84386 285 9

*Vanguard Press is an imprint of
Pegasus Elliot MacKenzie Publishers Ltd.*
www.pegasuspublishers.com

First Published in 2006

**Vanguard Press
Sheraton House Castle Park
Cambridge England**

Printed & Bound in Great Britain

For Brian, and in memory of Jimmy Logan.

Acknowledgements

For their efforts in helping me to complete the walk, I would like to thank the following:-

The villagers of Adfa for organising the Bingo night and for being so supportive; Tricia, Mary, Maria, Chris, Ann, Terry and Edwin for the free accommodation; Carris and Phyllis, and Neil and his fellow Milngavie Ramblers for their company; Beamer for boosting my self-confidence; Mike for his weekly phone calls; Duncan for taking on my unfinished work assignment; James for trying to get me some extra paid leave; all my colleagues at EDS (now transitioned to Capgemini) who sponsored me – especially those who helped to collect money (the use of ellipsis in the Introduction and final chapter may remind some of them of a certain former CEO . . .); all the friends, relations and complete strangers who contributed; all the B&B proprietors who gave me discounts, free dinners or packed lunches; Pauline for collecting money from her hairdressing clients; Marj and Sid for looking after the animals; and last but not least, Brian for all his support, both practical and emotional.

The total raised was £5250.

For their help in the production of this book, I would like to thank the following:-

Black and White Publishing for their very encouraging rejection letter; Maria and Mary for their supportive remarks; Alex Mabon for his emails; Julia for keeping the secret; Duncan and Paula for checking the proofs; and of course everyone at Pegasus for all their hard work and encouragement.

Charities that benefited were:

Severn Hospice Lymph-oedema Clinic

Hope House Children's Hospice

County Air Ambulance

Montgomeryshire Emergency Doctors

Accord Hospice

OCHRE

John O'Groats

Golspie

Drumnadrochit

Fort William

Crianlarich

Glasgow

Crawford

Gretna

Kendal

Malham Cove

Kinder Scout

Wolverhampton

Worcester

Bristol

Taunton

Okehampton

Land's End

CONTENTS

Introduction

Land's End is not the southernmost point of the British mainland – that honour is taken by Lizard Point, 35 miles away by road. It *is* the westernmost point of England, but *not* of mainland Britain – Ardnamurchan Point in the Highlands of Scotland is further west by half a degree of longitude (about 15 miles).

Similarly John O'Groats is not the northernmost point – Dunnet Head close by just manages to sneak ahead. The easternmost point of Britain is Lowestoft Point in East Anglia, the furthest point east in Scotland is at Peterhead, north of Aberdeen. Even in the far north-east, the furthest point east is Duncansby Head, two miles beyond John O'Groats.

So why Land's End to John O'Groats? Well it *is* corner to corner (sort of), and I suppose it has become traditional…

CHAPTER ONE

Memories
From the corners of my mind

It all started in about 1960, when I fell in love (the way teenage girls do) with an image on a TV screen. At that time, most girls were crazy about Elvis Presley or Cliff Richard (this was pre-Beatles). I had to be different, I chose instead a handsome young Scotsman who had his own show on TV at the time. I thought Jimmy Logan was gorgeous, and the best thing was that he appeared to be totally oblivious to the fact. Personally, there is nothing that turns me off quicker than a man who thinks he is God's gift to women – I could see the attraction in Elvis, but he knew exactly what effect he was having on all his female fans.

Even my mother approved of Jimmy Logan, to the extent that she wrote to him to ask about records he had made. She received a lovely letter in reply, which I still have, telling her about the 'Loganberry Pie' LP.

Coming from a show-business family, Jimmy Logan was born to be an entertainer. It was in his blood, and it was obvious how much he enjoyed his work. In the words of the song that he sang at the end of his show all those years ago:-
'It's been so nice tonight, just being with you,
I hope that you've enjoyed it half as much as I'.

That's all I can remember, but he meant every word. At the end he raised an arm in a farewell salute, and vanished, using the miracles of modern technology. In retrospect it was extremely primitive – you could actually see the square where they cut him out!

Well, that was more than forty years ago. The crush lasted two years and then I moved on. Subsequently, I had a crush on our maths teacher – known as Hank because he wore glasses like Hank Marvin from the Shadows – but that's a different story.

Fast-forward thirty-odd years, through marriage, two children and one grandchild to 1997. I have been a Computer

Programmer since 1974 (or Software Engineer, or Information Analyst, or whatever other title various employers seem to prefer). In 1997 I was working on a contract for Scottish Power in Paisley. One lunchtime I wandered down town for a mooch round the shops (a fairly regular occurrence). On the way I passed one of my favourite charity shops, in aid of the local hospice. The shop had been closed for some time for refurbishment. In the window was a big yellow poster announcing that the shop would be re-opened the following day by – guess who – none other than my childhood hero. I instantly fell in love all over again. It was a strange sensation – I felt as though I was thirteen again. Of course I went to the opening and got his autograph:-

"Can I have your autograph please?"

"Who shall I sign it to?"

"Kath."

"Is that with a K or a C?"

"K."

But I was too shy to have a proper conversation with him. I wanted to tell him about my teenage infatuation, but you can't walk up to a star and say 'I had a crush on you when I was thirteen', can you? Well *I* can't anyway, though I'm sure he would have been pleased.

The following week I went to his one-man show 'Laughter in the Aisles' at Paisley Methodist Church Hall, in aid of the aforementioned hospice. It was a wonderful evening of good clean family entertainment. He was on stage – alone – for a total of three hours, with songs, jokes and anecdotes spanning a lifetime in show business, the whole thing illustrated with slides and pieces of film. One highlight was an old piece of film of Sir Harry Lauder singing 'Roamin' in the Gloamin' in a theatre in the 1930s – the magical thing about this was that *both* audiences spontaneously sang along with the chorus, the present-day audience in the Methodist Church Hall joining in with the theatre audience of more than sixty years ago.

The measure of the man came when he was taking his bow after his encore (which was 'Keep right on to the end of the road'). Most entertainers, when they wish the applause to stop, will raise their hands. He kept his arms by his sides and just moved his fingers slightly – the applause stopped instantly. Every person in that packed hall was watching his every move, and loving every minute.

After enjoying the show so much, I decided to write a letter to the hospice, saying how much I had enjoyed seeing him and explaining about the crush. This had the desired effect – I received a lovely reply; they had enjoyed my letter so much that they had 'taken the liberty of sending it to him'. The following day a large envelope arrived – a signed photograph with a lovely personal letter from him saying that my letter was 'one of the nicest tributes I have had'.

Thus started a wonderful, never-ending, one-way love affair. My husband was jealous at first, until I explained that having an idol is a totally different thing from having a husband. Then it was "Oh, she's got a 'thing' about Jimmy Logan."

"But what has all this got to do with walking from Land's End to John O'Groats?" I hear you ask. You'll just have to be patient – clarification will come in a later chapter.

CHAPTER TWO

We parted on the shore

Yes, we parted on the shore,
I said "Goodbye my love,
And I'm off to Baltimore."

(Well no, John O'Groats actually)

Sunday 29/2/2004 Week 1

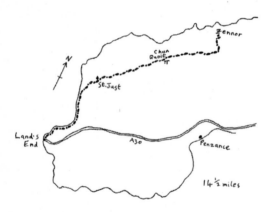

So here I am at Land's End, on a fine sunny morning. It is Sunday, 29th February 2004, which seems an appropriate date, as there is a definite air of unreality about the whole thing. Am I really going to walk all the way from here to the other end of the country in eight weeks? Well, that's the plan, and I hope I can see it through, especially as there is already a thousand pounds of sponsorship money in the bank.

    I am signing the official book of End-to-Enders, and my

husband is taking photos. Apparently about two-thousand people attempt the challenge every year. Of course they are not all walkers – many modes of transport are used, from horses to vintage cars, from tandems to motorised skips. The predominant method, however, is the bicycle, and then there are those who run all the way, the record currently being 9 days, 2 hours and 26 minutes, set in May 2002 by a friend of a work colleague. And I thought *I* was mad!

We drove down to Cornwall from Mid-Wales yesterday, or to be more precise, Brian drove. As we got into the car, he said, "You needn't think I'm going to drive all the way." So when we stopped at the services, I fully expected him to hand me the keys – instead he just got back into the driving seat, so I kept my mouth shut. There had been some concern about the weather as it had snowed a fair bit during the week, but once we got away from the slush-covered local roads there was nothing to hinder us. It is quite unusual for Cornwall to have snow, but Bodmin Moor was covered in a white blanket – the sledgers were out in force, taking advantage while they could.

You're probably wondering why I'm doing this walk at this time of year, when the weather could be harsh. Well, I'd rather walk in a hailstorm than a heatwave. I simply couldn't do it in the kind of hot weather we sometimes get in the summer – not even naked, like that chap last year. (He must have had lots of free lodgings though, mostly in police cells.) In March and April it should be not too hot, not too cold, and I shall be following the spring all the way North.

It is sunny with a cool breeze as we make our way to the famous signpost. 'John O'Groats 874', it proclaims – that is the shortest 'official' route, useful for record breakers but not very inspiring. My route will be about a hundred miles longer but I hope to see some interesting things and meet some interesting people along the way, and I won't be using roads any more than I have to – two legs have an advantage over two wheels in that respect. Okay, so I'm doing it for charity, but I'm also doing it for myself, and there's no point if I can't enjoy it. (It's only 602 miles as the crow flies, but I'm not a crow.)

I give Brian a big hug. "Will you marry me?" I ask (it being

29th February).

"No" he replies – dead romantic, my husband, though he is being very supportive, bless him. Then it's more photos, and video filming, which makes me feel very self-conscious, and I'm on my way. The Great Adventure has begun.

*

The first part of my route follows the South West Coastal Footpath, which is quite pleasant at this point. It is only a mile or two to Sennen Cove, where we had an excellent pub meal last night. I know Brian will be waiting for me there with his camcorder, so that he can film me some more before his long drive home. He will easily spot my bright yellow fleece, bought from a market stall five years ago, and perfect for this trip, with its high visibility and large zipped pockets. I'm right; he's there on the seafront, making me feel self-conscious again.

At this point I realise that I have forgotten about my sign. I fish it out and Brian helps me to pin it on to my rucksack. It is made from a piece of white cloth, with the outline of Britain on it and the words 'SPONSORED WALK, LE – JOG' in black. With a bit of luck it will generate some extra sponsorship cash from strangers.

We say "Goodbye, my love" – again – and off I go. The Coastal Footpath is now more varied, sometimes sandy paths, sometimes a scramble over rocks. My stick comes in useful at times. I wasn't going to bring one, as I've always been used to walking without, but Brian said "You're not going without a stick," and he made me a beautiful one, with a deer antler for a handle that I could use as a crutch in an emergency.

Many of the rocks are covered with a plant I've never seen before – it has masses of strange fleshy leaves and looks almost alien. At first I can't see any flowers on it, but then I spot one high up on a cliff – pink with many petals. When I look it up later (after the Adventure, as I'm not carrying heavy books), I discover it is called Hottentot Fig, a member of the Mesembryanthemum family, and is quite rare, only growing in a few places.

At St Just I leave the coast and head inland. There are shops here so I stock up on food – I'm staying in a hostel tonight, and it is self-catering at this time of year. My mobile phone rings – it's my daughter checking up on me. My two-month-old granddaughter is in hospital with some sort of viral infection, but she's getting better.

After leaving St Just, I head up across the moor. I still can't believe I'm walking to John O'Groats – it just feels like a good day out, a lovely Sunday walk. It reminds me of my sister-in-law, on the evening of her wedding day – "I don't feel like I've got married, I just feel as though I've had a really good day out, something special, somewhere different."

Chun Quoit is clear on the horizon at the top of Woon Gumpus Common, so it is easy to find my way up to it. This is an impressive Stone Age burial cairn, looking like a giant stone mushroom. It is built from four upright stone slabs that form a chamber, with a massive stone slab balanced on top at a slight angle. How did those primitive people manage it? There are several of these quoits in the area, but I don't have time to visit any more – I believe they are all very similar anyway.

A short way across the moor from Chun Quoit is Chun Castle, originally built over two-thousand years ago, now just a rough circular mound of ruined stonework, full of gorse bushes and brambles; the stones having been plundered for other uses.

Another recurring feature that litters the landscape of Cornwall is abandoned tin mines, the legacy of a four-thousand year old industry that became uneconomical. My route takes me close to a large one. It is quite an impressive square building, but is several hundred yards away across the moor, so I decide I need to conserve my energy – there probably wouldn't be much more to see when I got there. I am under the mistaken impression that it is the 'Men-an-Tol' marked on the map, but I later discover that Men-an-Tol is a round stone with a hole in the middle that is closer to the path but which I barely glance at. I really should have done more research before I started. There are many theories about the purpose of this strange stone, but who can guess what was in the minds of people long dead?

There are lots of paths criss-crossing over the moor, and

they are not all marked on the map. It is easy to take the wrong one, which I realise I have done and have to fight my way through a patch of gorse bushes to get back on course, scratching my legs in the process – my GPS (hand-held Global Positioning System) is useful here, to check my position. I go through an Iron Age settlement, but there is not much to see, just a group of rough mounds with cattle grazing among the stones and weeds.

Just before sunset I arrive at the village of Zennor. The Backpackers' Hostel is in an old chapel, and is basic but comfortable. It is not very busy – a few young people, mostly foreign – I feel a bit out of place. There is no signal on my mobile phone. I am under strict instructions to phone home every night so I have to use the payphone. I have a room with four bunk beds in it all to myself, so I make myself comfortable with an extra blanket and pillow, and sleep like a log.

CHAPTER THREE

I'm a rambler, I'm a rambler
From Manchester way

I developed a love of walking from an early age. Being born and bred, to the age of nine, in Eccles, Manchester, most of my early explorations involved city streets. I would walk the mile to school every day along the main street, window-shopping as I went and sometimes being late. The bus fetched me home at lunchtime, for a fare of three-ha'pence which my mother tied up in a hanky for safe keeping. The same window-shopping route got me back to school in the afternoon – I still prefer window-shopping to actually spending money – but after school (during the summer months anyway), I would find lots of different, more interesting, slightly longer walks. One of my favourites involved a section of canal towpath, part of the Bridgewater Canal. It was probably dirty and rather unsavoury, but being a city kid I didn't notice; in fact I found it fascinating. Horrors! – imagine allowing a seven – or eight-year-old to wander alone in such places nowadays!

(The Bridgewater Canal was the brainchild of the Duke of Bridgewater, who wanted an easy way to transport coal from his mines at Worsley into Manchester. It was the first industrial canal not to follow the route of a river, and was connected to the mines by a network of underground canals which stretched for miles on different levels. Eventually the Bridgewater ran for forty miles between Leigh and Runcorn, with no locks required. It included a stone aqueduct over the river Irwell at Barton, which was replaced later by the swing aqueduct over the Manchester Ship Canal.)

When I was a teenager, our parents took us (my brother and me) for walking holidays in the Lake District. It was an organised thing, in a big house with lots of other people. We went every Easter, and so did several other families, so it became quite a party. There would be a choice of 'A' or 'B' walks during the day, then dancing and games in the evening, after an excellent meal.

It is amazing how much the weather can vary at Easter. One year the rocks were covered with hoarfrost, which didn't melt all day, and formed interesting patterns – my brother took some fascinating photographs. Another year it was so hot that I cut the legs off an old pair of trousers to make shorts. Then there was the time that we climbed Skiddaw in a howling gale – it was raining horizontally and we had to lean into the wind to stay on our feet. I leant against the trig pillar on the summit and felt as though I was getting squashed. Conversation was impossible; you had to yell into the ear of a companion to make yourself heard. My waterproof plastic mac (I wasn't very well equipped in those days) was ripped to shreds by the force of the wind.

During the early years of marriage and childrearing there never seemed to be time for any serious walking, but as I got older I realised what I was missing, so I joined the newly formed local group of the Ramblers' Association. This was in Stonehaven, near Aberdeen, so we had plenty of beautiful Scottish countryside to explore on our fortnightly walks.

It is strange how you always remember the worst weather. On one of our early outings (our first coach trip), we drove up to Banff where we disembarked for a coastal walk in the pouring rain. We got soaked. At lunchtime we got back on the coach to eat, then drove a bit further and dutifully trouped out into the rain for an afternoon walk. Sylvia, one of our members, said "Well at least we'll remember it!" Years later when we were discussing it, we decided that if we had all known each other better at the time, someone would have had the sense to suggest that we should just go home after lunch.

One of the best walks that I remember was a circuit of Loch Muich. It was a beautiful clear sunny day in September, the sky was a brilliant blue and it wasn't too hot – perfect walking weather. The views were amazing, and high on a hillside near the top end of the loch, a red deer stag stood guard over it all. As we were relaxing over lunch at the head of the loch, Annabel said, "Right now I don't envy a soul – not a soul." The remarkable thing is that it stays in my memory as an excellent walk, even though I had raging toothache all day!

I may be a wage slave on Monday,
But I am a free man on Sunday.

* M o n d a y   1 / 3 / 2 0 0 4 *

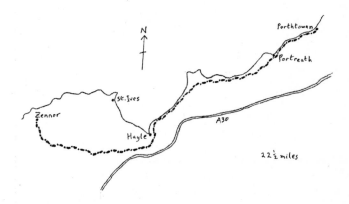

I wake early on the second day of the Adventure, and after a quick breakfast of bread and cheese I leave the hostel just as the sun is rising. It is St David's Day, so I pick a daffodil from the wayside and attach it to the strap of my rucksack. My shoulders are aching a bit from the unaccustomed weight. It's not really very heavy, only about 15lb – it's amazing what you can manage without. This is what I am carrying, in a 20-litre rucksack:-

Lightweight waterproofs
Spare trousers
2 pairs walking socks
2 pairs knickers
Bra
T-shirt
Boxer shorts (to wear at night with T-shirt at hostels)
Over-shirt (extra layer when required)
Lightweight canvas shoes
2 pairs thin socks

Warm hat and gloves
Sponge-bag (containing just the essentials)
Towel (very small)
Small first aid kit
Maps (photocopies of OS maps up to the Midlands)
Notebooks (one for diary, one with list of addresses and phone numbers)
Cheque book
Torch (the size of a lipstick but very powerful)
Spare films
Pills (HRT, cod liver oil and glucosamine sulphate)
Spectacles
Charger for mobile phone
Thermal cushion (for sitting on cold or damp ground)
Survival bag (just in case)
Variable amounts of food

Brian wanted me to bring a small tent for emergencies, but I said that was too heavy so we compromised on the survival bag (which only weighs 10oz) – I sincerely hope I don't have to use it. In the pockets of my trousers I have a purse, camera, personal alarm, compass, GPS and a pen. The pockets of my fleece contain my mobile phone, bottle of water, Lucozade, chocolate bar, and an apple, for quick refreshment on the move.

I adjust the straps of my rucksack and carry on. My toes were a bit sore this morning so I took the advice of the 'experts' and put on a thin pair of socks under my thick walking socks. Big mistake! I head across country by way of narrow lanes and muddy tracks to Nuncledra. There are still pockets of snow in some of the sheltered hedgerows. Then it's roads to the seaside town of Hayle, where I stop for something to eat and send a text to my daughter – the baby is okay, coming home today.

Here I make my second big mistake. Hayle has a beautiful level beach, about three miles long, which would be very pleasant to walk along. Instead I follow the way-marked Coastal path, which winds through the sand dunes, in and out, up and down, playing havoc with my feet and adding at least a mile to the journey. By the time I reach Gwithian at the far end of the beach, my toes are very painful and I have to stop and take my boots off. After removing both pairs of socks and stashing the thin pair in my rucksack, I attend to my blisters. There's a really nasty one, with blood in it, at the base of the little toenail. I drain it and put on a toe protector. Several others also need attention. Overall, this first aid takes half an hour, but it is well worth it as my feet are much more comfortable now. Unfortunately it is now half-past two; sunset is at six o'clock, and I still have at least ten miles to go.

Much as I would like to explore the Coastal footpath some more, common sense prevails and I follow the road, which runs parallel to the coast and is kinder to the feet, for several miles to Portreath. Now I have three choices to get to tonight's destination at Porthtowan: the Coastal footpath, which could be hard work, a long diversion by road, or a track leading to Nancekuke Common, with an 'airfield (disused)' according to the map.

As it looks like the shortest and easiest route, I decide on the latter, in the hope of being able to cross the airfield unhindered. If this fails, I can divert to the Coastal footpath. The road uphill is simple enough, but when I reach the 'airfield' I am met by an enormous wire fence plastered with notices 'MOD – KEEP OUT' with suitable penalties for infringement. Obviously not a viable route!

I find out later that this is RAF Portreath, formerly CDE (Chemical Defence Establishment) Nancekuke – a top-secret site for research and production of chemical weapons.

Keeping the wire to my right, I cross a couple of fields and turn on to the Coastal footpath. The wire continues on my right for quite a long way, and with the cliffs down to the sea on my left, I wonder what will happen to the footpath when the sea erodes the cliffs – will the Ministry of Defence agree to move the fence back a few yards?

The path is quite easy apart from some deep gullies, which would be a lot worse without the man-made steps. They're still hard work after a long, tiring day. I have just reached the bottom of one when I see a young woman coming down the other side – she stands to one side of the steps to let me pass. "Are there

33

many more of these between here and Porthtowan?" I ask. She tells me there is only one more but it's worse than this one, and she reckons I should get there before dark. She says she would give me a donation but she hasn't got any money on her, so she wishes me good luck and I continue on my way. Just as the sun is setting a man passes me in the other direction – he has a huge rucksack so he must be intending to camp somewhere soon, the path wouldn't be safe in the dark. The light is fading as I arrive in Porthtowan, where I am greeted by a very friendly B&B landlady, with a hot bath and a plate of stew. She lets me use her phone to call Brian as there is no signal on the mobile again.

Tuesday 2/3/2004

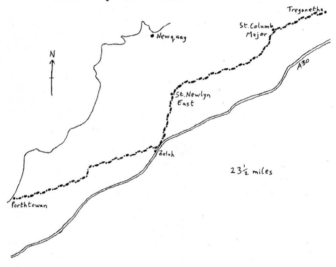

The next morning she gives me an early breakfast, as I have another long day ahead of me. I make some changes to my planned route, to stay mainly on roads, as rough footpaths can be hard on the toes. So, saying goodbye to the Coastal footpath, I head inland. My mother phones to see how I'm getting on – she doesn't believe I can do it, I tell her I *will* – I always did have a stubborn streak, she should remember that.

My route takes me through several villages. At Mithian I have a brief rest on a bench, and watch two horse-riders make their way through the village. Near Gollawater a group of flower-pickers are busy in a large field of daffodils. It is nice to see lots of young green plants poking their way through the ground in the hedgerows. Most are impossible to identify at this stage, but there are plenty of primroses and celandines flowering already. After Zelah I have to walk along the main A30 for half a mile – not pleasant.

The small town of St Newlyn East has public toilets, which are very convenient (!), but I don't see a shop. Just up the road is the Lappa Valley Steam Railway, which is of course closed this early in the year, so there's not much to see. There are now several miles of country road before the next town.

It is five o'clock as I come into St Columb Major, and there are still about four miles to go, so I phone my B&B to say I won't be there till after sunset. This is a pleasant town, but some of the drivers are lunatics, screeching round the narrow streets without a thought for mere pedestrians. Three young boys are messing about on bikes on the pavement in front of me. One falls off and seems pleasantly surprised that his mobile phone is not broken. As I pass them they notice my 'Sponsored Walk' sign and shout after me, "Are you a boy or a girl?"

"I'm a lady." They start asking me questions – kids today are so uninhibited.

"Are you trying to get into the record books?"

"No, I'm just trying to make some money for charity."

"Can we come with you?"

"I don't think so!"

They accompany me as far as the main road that bypasses the town, where I manage to persuade them not to come any further.

It has been a long hard slog today, and the last three miles to Tregonetha take all my willpower. It is dark when I get there and I have to ask directions. I soak my weary feet in a hot bath while my landlady rustles up an omelette and chips.

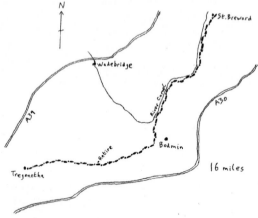

In the morning she gives me a donation and advises me on the footpath across the fields. Some of these footpaths look fine on the map but can be quite hard to follow on the ground. She says this one is okay so I try it, but go wrong somewhere and have to negotiate a barbed-wire fence and some brambles before I get back on track. It was overcast at breakfast time and now it is raining – the first time in four days – enough to make me don my waterproof jacket, but I won't bother with the trousers as it's only a heavy drizzle.

I now follow pleasant country roads towards Bodmin. A signpost points to 'RETIRE' – is it trying to tell me something? There's no way I'm giving up at this early stage, despite blisters and aching knees. It's a shorter day today, only sixteen miles – yesterday was twenty-three.

I need to stock up on food, so I make a diversion to the main road at Bodmin, where I find a petrol station which fulfils my requirements.

North of Bodmin, the Camel Trail follows the course of an old railway line, close to the river Camel. Old railway tracks converted to paths are always pleasant to walk along, being smooth, level, reasonably straight, and peaceful away from the roads. This one is no exception and I find it most enjoyable, even though it is still raining slightly. I look down on the river, where a series of weirs has been built by the Bodmin Anglers Association to improve the fishing. They received a national conservation award for this work.

Where the trail crosses a road, the railway tracks are still visible, embedded in the tarmac. At the end of the trail at Poley's Bridge, there is a large metal sculpture of a fish – I'm not sure of the significance of this, but it's very impressive. Unfortunately the rain becomes much heavier as I continue by road to my lodgings at St Breward. There doesn't seem much point in putting on the waterproof trousers at this late stage, so I am quite wet when I arrive. I strip off and have a shower – there is no bath here.

I send my daughter a text message so that she can phone me for a chat – it's cheaper for her to phone me as she is on a contract whereas I am pay-as-you-go.

Thursday 4/3/2004

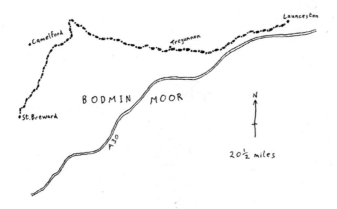

For some reason, I feel nervous this morning. Perhaps I am beginning to realise that I am actually *doing* this, and there's an awful long way to go in the next seven-and-a-half weeks. It's best not to think about that, just concentrate on today's journey. After an excellent breakfast and a friendly chat with the landlady, who gives me a donation, I feel more confident and set off into a misty morning. Pleasant country roads with smooth grass verges lead me round the north-west edge of Bodmin Moor, and the mist soon clears.

I was hoping to cut across Davidstow woods, but there is no access so I have to go round. Now I am on an unfenced road crossing a huge airfield to the north of the moor. It is hard to tell whether it is still used – the control tower looks semi-derelict, but there is still a windsock. The Davidstow cheese factory is behind me on the horizon.

Before starting the walk, I contacted all the groups of the Ramblers' Association that are close to my route, suggesting that some of their members might like to accompany me for sections of the walk. The response was limited, but I did get a few offers of accommodation. One of these is in Worcester. As I am walking across the airfield, a friend of my benefactress, who works for their local hospice, phones me to arrange some publicity when I pass through Worcester.

A long straight road leads downhill towards Launceston. An inn called the 'Rising Sun' is advertising lunches, so I go in for a meal. The only other customers are three oldish gentlemen sitting at the bar chatting to the barmaid. They spot my sign and show an interest. After asking lots of questions they give me some money, including some "from the landlady – I'll get it back off her."

"Do you know her well?"

"Well enough to get £2 off her." It's not often you come out of a pub with more money than when you went in.

I pass through a small village called Tregunnon, which is odd, because I live near a village in Wales called Tregynon, that is pronounced the same even though it is spelt differently. I suppose it's because the Cornish language and Welsh have the same roots. The village of Polyphant has a beautiful old house that looks as though it needs some first aid, or even major surgery, with broken windows and a hole in the roof. There are building materials lying about, but it doesn't look as though any work has been done for a while.

The old town of Launceston welcomes me about teatime and I am happy to find that my guest house has a bath. After settling in, I change into my canvas shoes and hobble down the road to get a meal from the nearest chip shop. It's funny how hard it is to walk in the evening – my knees seem to seize up when I stop. Once I have eaten, I have my diary to write and phone calls to make, including one to an old friend in Taunton who is putting me up in four days' time. She tells me where to find the key to let myself in and make myself at home if I get there before she gets back from work.

I keep my mobile switched on all night so that I can use it as an alarm clock – tonight it disturbs me in the middle of the night with a text message from T-mobile informing me that my calls will be cheaper for the rest of the month because I have used ten pounds-worth of credit. Also the bed has a waterproof cover to protect the mattress, which makes me very hot and sweaty.

* F r i d a y 5 / 3 / 2 0 0 4 *

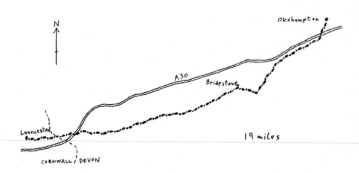

My planned route today would take me through Lifton and Chillaton to join an old railway line converted to a cycle track at Lydford. This route could be quite steep in places. After discussing it with my landlady, I decide to use the old A30 (now an unclassified road) instead. She says it is quite pleasant to walk along.

Launceston is the gateway to Cornwall, of which it was the ancient capital. It is Cornwall's only walled town, and was once the home of the Royal Mint. As I leave I look behind me and have a good view of the Castle, built by the first Norman Earl of Cornwall, that dominates the town.

Shortly after leaving Launceston, I cross the River Tamar into Devon – it has taken me five days just to get through Cornwall. The phone rings – it is Mike, an old buddy from work, phoning to see how I'm getting on. We're no longer in the same team but we keep in touch, sharing a love of cryptic crosswords. A few miles further on, Duncan, a team member, also phones.

The landlady was right about the old A30, it is a nice quiet road, straight and level. In the small town of Lewdown the road is being re-surfaced, a convoy system with an escort vehicle in operation for the traffic. It is great to be free of the hassles of motoring. I turn to go through Bridestow so that I can join up with the afore-mentioned cycle track, passing a road called 'Pig's Leg Lane' on the way. The place I choose for getting onto the track is not an official access point, and I find myself scrambling down a steep bank in order to avoid a detour.

From here it is easy walking, but it seems a long way into Okehampton. As I arrive in the town I get a text from my daughter – 'Left right left right quick march'. I am having trouble finding the street where the B&B is – it's amazing how people who have lived in a town all their lives don't know the names of the streets. It is getting dark and starting to rain, so I phone up and the lady of the house comes to meet me. She and her husband make me feel really at home, providing refreshments, a hot bath to soak my aching knees (they're really bad tonight), and an invitation to join them in their sitting room later (where I notice that the wallpaper is exactly the same as ours).

The plan was to stay at the Youth Hostel tonight, but it was fully booked. I'm quite glad really – you wouldn't get hospitality like this at a hostel, nor a wonderful cooked breakfast; and certainly not a donation to your cause.

Brian is in hospital today, having an arthroscopy – keyhole surgery on his knee to trim the cartilage. I phone him there and he seems okay – he'll only be staying in overnight. His sister and brother-in-law are staying at our house for a few days to look after the dogs and the pony.

The days are settling into a routine now. Before I started, I thought that I would walk six miles in two hours then rest for half an hour, continuing like that throughout the day. It's not working out that way. In the first place, I seem to be walking slower than usual, only doing about five miles in two hours. Secondly, whenever I stop my knees seize up and it's hard to get going again. Once I've got going I'm okay, so I just plod on like the tortoise in the fable, only stopping for lunch either at a pub or cafe, or using supplies from my bag, which I replenish when I see a suitable shop.

In the evening, the first thing to do is to remove my rucksack and boots – however comfortable the boots are, it is wonderful to take them off at the end of a long day. Then, after accepting any hospitality that is offered, I do an ET (phone home!). The next task – vitally important this one – is to examine my feet and deal with any new blisters, smothering them with E45 cream after a bath or shower and letting them breathe until the morning, when I will treat them with surgical spirit and put on toe protectors and plasters where necessary. A small amount of laundry needs to be done every day – at this time of year the radiators are on, so it dries easily after rolling it in a towel to remove excess water.

Then I have to get a meal. Some B&Bs provide evening meals, but they tend to be rather expensive and I am trying to keep my expenditure to a minimum. In a town there is usually a fish and chip shop or a pub quite nearby. Failing this I have to rely on my own supplies. This is no great hardship – I usually have a full cooked breakfast that sets me up for the day, and sometimes I can get a cooked meal at lunchtime. A Pot Noodle is a handy thing to carry as it is lightweight and only needs boiling water to provide a hot meal, although rather uninteresting.

Having satisfied my hunger, I turn my attention to a review

of my situation. I check how far ahead I have booked my accommodation, study my maps and lists of addresses, and make any necessary phone calls. It is vital to be several days ahead of myself, so that I don't have any worries and can concentrate on the actual walk. Before I started I booked the first five nights, and I am trying to stay at least three days ahead. Then I must write my diary, otherwise I would forget all the details of this wonderful experience. I also make a list of the photos I have taken, and measure the route I took today, using a piece of ribbon marked out in miles.

Saturday 6/3/2004

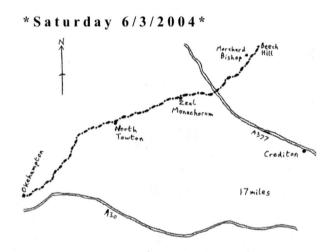

After a friendly farewell I head into town for a visit to the supermarket, then go to the chemist to get two elastic knee supports. The young assistant is very helpful, measuring my knees to get the right size, and I put them on there and then. Hopefully they will ease the aches a little.

A pleasant country road takes me up to Sampford Courtenay and across to North Tawton. Just by the cheese factory a man in a car stops and gives me five pounds. He has a boy with him and we chat for a while. He says the boy's mother lives in Lairg, which is not far from John O'Groats, and it takes two days by car, so he can appreciate what I'm doing.

From the road to Zeal Monachorum you can see for miles and miles – the edge of Dartmoor to the south and standard English farmland to the north. Devon soil is very red. Zeal Monachorum means 'cell of the monks'. It is a very pretty little village, but it is rather spoilt at the moment by large-scale repairs to the water mains – all these holes in the road must make it very difficult for traffic.

As I approach the village of Down St Mary, the six church bells are being rung up – raised gradually from hanging to an upright position in readiness for proper ringing. One of them fails to 'stand', continuing to ring for a couple of strokes after the others have stopped. After a pause they start ringing a method, and must be attempting a peal or quarter-peal because I can hear them continuously until they are out of earshot. It makes me quite nostalgic – I used to do a lot of bell ringing years ago.

A bit further up the road are some excellent public conveniences – it's nice not to have to look for a hedge for a change. From here I had intended to follow the Two Moors Way, but I decide it will be simpler just to use the roads as they're pleasant enough.

Tonight I am staying at Beech Hill Community near Morchard Bishop. I'm not sure what to expect as I approach a large, old, rambling house down a long drive. I am welcomed and shown to a room with a piece of paper pinned to the plain wooden door declaring this to be the bed and breakfast room. After being shown where the toilet and shower are, and told there is a bath upstairs, I am taken to the communal kitchen, which has a big wooden table with benches either side. One of the residents is celebrating her fortieth birthday, so they offer me a slice of banoffee pie. There are about ten people living here. They all work part-time to pay the bills, but try to be as self-sufficient as possible, keeping chickens, growing vegetables, and doing all their own maintenance. Everyone is very friendly, and the accommodation is cheap, basic but very comfortable. I decide not to go upstairs for a bath, as stairs are so hard on the knees. They tell me I should get a signal on the mobile phone if I go up to the woodpile – Brian is home from the hospital now and doing fine.

As I'm getting ready for bed I hear a scuffling noise – it sounds as though it's coming from the chest of drawers. I open the top drawer and discover some chocolate wrappers and the remains of chocolate raisins with all the chocolate nibbled off!

Sunday 7/3/2004 Week 2

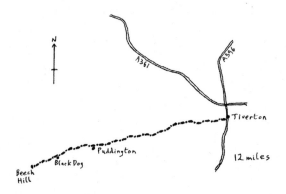

At breakfast time I am thrilled to discover that the residents have held a collection for me. Most of them have either gone to work or are going about their day's chores. My fried eggs are the freshest I have had for years – you can really taste the difference – and the home-made crab apple jelly is superb. Before I go I leave a note in the bedroom – 'Thanks for everything. Check the top drawer, I think you've got some little furry friends!'

It's a nice short day today; only about twelve miles – the shortest yet. I follow country lanes through Black Dog, Puddington, and Pennymoor, but I can't find a pub open at lunch time. There are lots of military aircraft about, and a helicopter which appears to be following me (of course it's not really; my imagination is working overtime). The pretty blue flowers of periwinkles are growing in the hedgerows. I get a text message

44

from Pauline, the teacher at my evening art class; she's checking on my progress. I'm going to miss a few classes. Later I lean on a gate to phone my daughter for a chat.

When I arrive at the guest house in Tiverton there is a note on the door – 'back at 4:30'. It's only 3:15 so I explore the town centre. It has a very nice pedestrian area with lots of charity shops – what a pity it's Sunday and they're all closed. It's just as well though, I wouldn't be able to carry any purchases. I sit on a bench in the sun and phone Brian. My ten-year-old granddaughter in Aberdeen has her mobile phone switched off, so I leave a voice mail.

After settling in at the guest house, I go out for a pizza. On the way back the church bells are ringing, and there is a beautiful sunset. My granddaughter sends a text, so I phone her back for a chat.

"Where are you?"

"Tiverton."

"Where's that?"

"Get your Dad to show you on the road atlas."

The Youth Hostel at Cheddar has the answer phone on, so I can't book. It would have been an interesting place to visit, but after studying the maps I realise I can cut out some miles by going straight up through Wells, so I book a night at Chew Stoke, leaving eight miles into Bristol the following day. That will feel like a day off.

CHAPTER FOUR

So if you really love me
Come on and let it show

Jimmy Logan was diagnosed with oesophageal cancer in September 2000. At the time he was starring in 'The Golden Years of Harry Lauder' at Pitlochry Festival Theatre. He wanted his performance to be judged on its merits, without a sympathy factor (he got rave reviews), so his illness was not publicised until October – probably only in the Scottish media. In any case, I didn't find out about it until the following February. I was browsing the Internet when I came across a report about it in the *Daily Record*. It was an old report, and I was worried that he might have died meantime without me hearing about it, so I phoned the *Daily Record* to enquire. The lady I spoke to said,

"Oh, I think his funeral was last Friday."

"You mean he's dead?"

Then she realised she had got it wrong; it was Jack Milroy (another Scottish comedian) who had died, and she apologised for upsetting me.

On 8th March 2001, a variety concert was staged at the Pavilion Theatre in Glasgow. It was called 'A Celebration for Jimmy Logan'. He was so well-loved in Glasgow that the tickets sold out in four hours – a record for the Pavilion. All the artistes gave their services free, and the show raised £30,000 for charity. The concert was filmed, and a video (of which I have a copy) was made of the highlights. It was certainly a very emotional evening, as everyone was aware that it was probably his last public appearance. Five weeks later, on 13th April – Good Friday – he died peacefully in hospital.

A few months later, in the autumn, I was browsing the Internet again. I found an article – I think it was another newspaper report – about a charity called Ochre. Its patron is Sean Connery and it supports people with oesophageal cancer, but the article didn't say much about it as it was mostly about

Sean Connery. I had an email conversation with someone who advised me to phone Jimmy Logan's widow, Angela. She came down from a stepladder (she was replacing a light bulb) to talk to me about Ochre. It stands for 'Oesophageal Cancer Has Reached Everywhere', and was started by a Glasgow doctor who had had oesophageal cancer but had beaten it – it can be cured if diagnosed soon enough. She also told me that they were planning to plant a tree in Jimmy's memory. It was to be a flowering cherry tree, and would be planted in the middle of a rose garden in Glasgow's Botanic Gardens. I said I thought that was a lovely idea.

The following spring I was driving to work and playing a Troggs CD (I have eclectic tastes). One of their best songs, from 1967, is 'Love is All Around', which was a big hit for Wet Wet Wet many years later. Just as it came to the line 'So if you really love me, come on and let it show', I passed a cherry tree in full bloom. I immediately thought about Jimmy Logan's tree. It was at this moment that I decided that I had to get serious about my plans for a Sponsored Walk. The way he faced up to his cancer, turned it around and made something positive out of it, was an inspiration. If he could raise thousands of pounds for charity when he was dying, then surely I can do something while I'm fit and healthy – I have to 'come on and let it show'.

Monday 8/3/2004

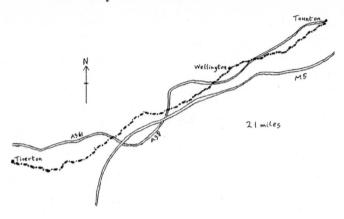

Most B&Bs are quite flexible with breakfast times, so if I've got a long day I can have it early. Here it is 8:00 to 8:30. The only advantage of this is that you get to meet some of the other guests. By coincidence there are two men here who are attempting the same trek as me. They are retired so can take a bit more time over it than me. They started two days before I did and are planning to do it in eleven weeks. Tonight they are just going to Wellington, whereas I am going a few miles further, to Taunton.

Another cycle track along an old railway takes me out of the town, then I join the towpath of the Grand Western Canal. That helicopter is still following me! The walkers from the guest house overtake me, and I catch them up later when they stop for a rest at Sampford Peverell. It's like the hare and the tortoise.

At Westleigh I leave the canal and take country roads through Sampford Moor and Wellington to Taunton, where I let myself in to my friend's house and help myself to a glass of milk and a piece of cake. Tricia gets home half an hour later. We were at university together many years ago, before I dropped out to get married. We haven't seen each other for years, so we have a lot to catch up on. She puts my washing in the machine while I have a bath.

Her husband, Mike, has an interesting photo-map of

Taunton. He shows me the best route through the town centre for the morning. I ask him if he knows what the footpath along the River Tone is like (part of tomorrow's route), but he's never walked it.

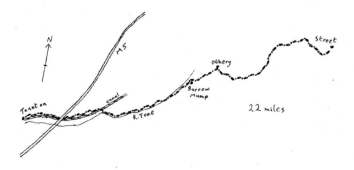

I leave Tricia's house just as they are leaving (separately) to go to work. They both offer me a lift into town – "No thanks, that would be cheating." In the centre of Taunton a bridge crosses the River Tone, and here I get onto the riverbank where the Somerset Space Walk starts. This is effectively a scale model of the Solar System, spread along the towpath of the Bridgwater and Taunton Canal for twelve miles, each planet represented by a ball of the appropriate size housed in a concrete pillar, at the correct relative distance from the other planets. Here in Taunton is Pluto, made from stainless steel and about the size of a pea.

The canal towpath is pleasant walking for a few miles. At Charlton I leave the canal and rejoin the River Tone. There is an excellent footpath with easily-opened gates – I'll have to tell Mike. There are a lot of shells along the riverbank. They look like some sort of freshwater clam, about the size of duck eggs but in two halves. A pair of swans are mating on the river – I can't get my camera out quickly enough. Further along, a big machine is harvesting the willows. They are stacked on the bank like a row of wigwams. Where I leave the river at Curload, there is a business selling willows. It has a big yard with stacks of different types, just like a timber yard.

A straight road goes north-east for two miles, with cottages spread out all along it. One has a shed with a painted trellis and painted flowers – a bright splash of colour all year round. This is Athelney, where legend has it that King Alfred burnt the cakes.

At Burrowbridge I sit on a bench outside a closed pub to eat my bread and cheese. Mary, who is putting me up in Worcester, phones to say that she is going away for the weekend but will be back before I get there – she was worried that I might think she'd done a runner if I phoned and got no answer.

Nearby Burrow Mump (lovely name!) is an eighty-foot high natural mound with the ruined church of St Michael on top. Royalist soldiers took refuge here during the Civil War.

From Othery (where the shop is closed) to Street is a long walk across the flat, open moor land of the Somerset Levels. Roads and ditches cross the moor in a grid pattern that I need to negotiate diagonally. There are some footpaths but they don't look very inviting, so I keep to the roads and proceed in a zigzag fashion.

Just this side of Street is Walton Hill. On it is an old windmill painted white, but no longer with sails. You can see it for miles. It's mocking me, trying to tell me 'not far now – you can see me so it can't be far'. It doesn't fool me, I know its still miles. In the far distance I can also see a hill with a monument on top, and wonder what it is. Later I realise it is Glastonbury Tor, which I will be passing tomorrow.

One of the roads has a sign – 'Road liable to subsidence'. About half way along, three ENORMOUS tractors with ENORMOUS trailers go past, and the ground shakes under my feet. The sun is getting low in the sky as I approach the windmill. It turns everything golden – you'd almost think it was autumn. Although the days are getting longer, and sunrise is much earlier, sunset is still shortly after six o'clock, almost the same as it was over a week ago. This puzzles me for a while, until I realise it is because I am travelling eastwards, closer to the Greenwich Meridian.

An overgrown bridle track takes me up past the windmill to a nasty main road just as it's starting to get dark. From the safety of a car park I phone my B&B and am given excellent directions. A girl in the car park asks me if I'm lost, and warns me about a blind corner on the road. There is no footpath and the road is busy, so I am glad to come off it and drop down into Street, where my landlady helps me get my boots off, and gives me milk and mince pies (presumably left over from Christmas).

There is no TV here, which is unusual at a B&B, but perhaps it is just as well, as I have a lot of phone calls to make. I am having trouble finding anywhere to stay between Bristol and Gloucester. My original intention was to follow the Severn Way from Avonmouth to Gloucester, but B&Bs seem to be few and far between in this area, or at least, *advertised* ones are rare. For Friday night I want somewhere in the Oldbury-on-Severn area, but everywhere I phone is either full or doesn't do B&B any more. Eventually I find a hotel in Almondsbury that can book me a bed, but can't supply breakfast on Saturday morning. For Saturday night I had hoped to book at the Youth Hostel in Slimbridge, but it is full, as are all the B&Bs I can find in Slimbridge or Frampton-on-Severn. My landlady comes to the rescue with reference books, and I make a list of addresses in Dursley. Unfortunately it is too late to phone them tonight.

Wednesday 10/3/2004

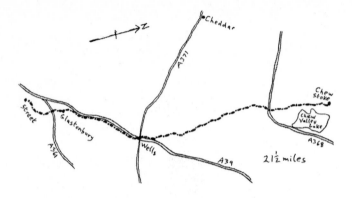

In the morning I succeed in booking a B&B in Dursley. It is a bit expensive, but sounds very comfortable, with underfloor heating in the en suite bathroom. It is close enough to Slimbridge that I will be able to rejoin my preferred route on Sunday.

My landlady promises to send me a donation if I write to her when I get to John O'Groats. She also gives me some moleskin to try on my blisters – this is a sticky piece of fabric that can be cut up as required and stuck on to provide a protective second skin. I'll try some tomorrow.

I skirt round the east side of Street and head north to Glastonbury. On the way I get halfway up a farm track that should be a short-cut, but have to turn back when I am told that it is private.

There are many legends about Glastonbury Tor – is it the home of the fairy folk? Or of Gwyn ap Nudd, the Lord of the Underworld? Or even of King Arthur? Believe whatever you want to believe. The site was certainly used by ancient religions, in later centuries being taken over by Christians.

Even the purpose of the terracing round the hill is disputed – is it a sacred labyrinth, or is it just a series of agricultural terraces raised above the surrounding floodplain?

The Tor is very impressive, whatever its origins – however

I don't have time to examine it at close quarters. I buy food in the town and continue up the main road, much of which has a cycle track alongside. It is part of route 3 of the National Cycle Network.

Arriving in Wells, I find a small cafe for lunch. The waitress and some of the customers show an interest in what I am doing, but no donations are forthcoming – never mind, it's nice to be wished 'good luck'. I pause for a few minutes to admire the cathedral – what a magnificent building! I wouldn't have seen it if I had stuck to my original route through Cheddar.

As I leave the town I think about the cathedral, and similar ones round the country. Vast sums of money were spent on building them – it seems somewhat immoral that the Church should have been so rich in an age when so much of the population was living hand-to-mouth. But on second thoughts, many labourers and craftsmen were required for such projects, so people were thereby able to earn an honest living, often for a lifetime.

It is now a long hard slog up country roads to Chew Stoke. I was hoping to visit the caves at Wookey Hole, but there isn't time if I am going to get to my B&B before dark. Here it is over 250 metres above sea-level, and it is trying to snow. The advantage of snow, of course, is that it is not as wet as rain. Near Chew Valley Lake is a road sign, a standard red warning triangle, with a picture of a duck – not one I've seen before!

It is dusk when I arrive at my B&B – it's been another long one today. There is no signal on my mobile so the landlord lets me use his phone to call Brian, but it is engaged for ages. Eventually I get through and find he has been chatting to a friend.

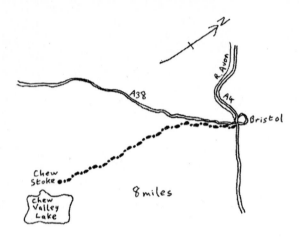

At breakfast, two men from Cumbria are enjoying a hearty meal. They are contractors working on a communications mast in the area. I discuss today's route with the landlord. I was planning to use part of the Monarch's Way, but he tells me the waymarking is not very good, and that the path is quite rough in places with lots of stiles to climb. I don't think my knees will cope with that, so I decide to stick to the roads. He also shows me on the map where a good cycle track leads from the suburbs into the centre of Bristol.

It is a cold, dampish sort of day, with flurries of snow, but they don't settle. There's no hurry today as it's only eight miles. My road takes me north up a steep hill to Maiden Head, then downhill again into Withywood on the edge of Bristol. I eat a chocolate bar and look for a litter bin but instead I find a workman picking up litter so I put my rubbish into his bin on wheels and have a chat with him.

The cycle track is a pleasant way of getting through the suburbs. Brian was worried about me walking through city streets, but this is okay. By the time I reach the city centre, my knee is aching quite badly, even though it's only been eight miles today. I do some shopping at the supermarket and arrive at the Youth Hostel at two o'clock. It would be nice to explore the city, but I need a rest, so I spend the whole afternoon sitting in my bunk (on the fifth floor!) with my feet up, writing my diary, checking my maps, and talking to family and friends. By evening I am feeling better, so I go down to the kitchen and cook myself a meal, then spend the rest of the evening in the TV lounge. There is an interesting programme about the dinosaur, Tyrannosaurus Rex – was he a predator or a scavenger? The conclusion is that he was a bit of both.

* F r i d a y   1 2 / 3 / 2 0 0 4 *

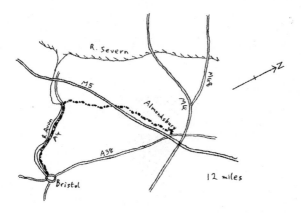

It has snowed in the night and there is a thin layer everywhere, but it is melting fast. There is a good view of the rooftops of Bristol from this fifth-floor window. The two girls who I shared a room with are planning to cycle from here to London in three days. They have bought some fancy drinking bottles with tubes, and are trying to work out how to use them. After chatting, I go down to breakfast – Bristol Youth Hostel is one of the few that include a full breakfast in the price – it is self-service so I make sure I have plenty.

The weather is very gloomy as I walk beside the Floating Harbour. This is not, as you might think, a harbour that floats, but rather a harbour where the water level is kept constant by means of locks, so that boats can always float in it.

Within the harbour is the SS Great Britain, the world's first ocean-going propeller-driven iron ship, launched in 1843. It was designed by Isambard Kingdom Brunel and built in Bristol, and was brought back home for restoration after being abandoned in the Falkland Islands. It's on the other side of the river so I don't pay it a visit.

Brunel also designed the Clifton Suspension Bridge, which I am approaching now. The building of the bridge was beset by problems, and it wasn't completed until 1864, thirty-five years after it was first proposed, and five years after Brunel's death. The bridge seems to be almost in the clouds on this murky day – I've seen it looking much better in photographs.

Below the bridge, at the base of the cliff, is the entrance of the Clifton Rocks Railway. Built in the 1890s as a short cut up the hill to Clifton, this was a financial disaster and finally closed in 1922. During the Second World War the tunnel was used as an emergency studio by the BBC.

After passing under the bridge, I continue along the main road beside the River Avon. I wore my warm hat this morning for the first time, but now I am too hot so I take it off. At Sea Mills I am studying an information board when my mate Mike from work phones to check up on me – this looks like it's going to be a regular Friday morning event. From here a pleasant footpath takes me away from the streets, up through Coombe Dingle to Blaise Estate, where some children are playing in a play park. I sit and watch them while I eat my lunch. Then it's rather dull roads through Hallen and Easter Compton to Almondsbury. It's a pity the weather is so gloomy because you should be able to see the 'old' and 'new' Severn bridges from here, even though they are about five miles away. It is totally overcast and not exactly misty, but visibility is very poor. In this area there are a lot of houses with electronic gates and burglar alarms – someone tells me later that this is the richest parish in the country.

When I find my hotel I go into the bar to book in, and am given a key to a room in a separate building. It's more like a motel room really, very basic but comfortable. It's a double room with an en suite bathroom, and is the same price whether there's one or two in it.

Tonight the village hall at home in Adfa is holding a Bingo Night and Auction Sale to raise funds for me – apparently bingo is the best money-spinner. I'm glad they're doing it while I'm away as I hate bingo! It's wonderful that they are being so supportive.

After having a bath and relaxing for a while I go back to the bar to get a meal. As I walk in, a man in a wheelchair who I'd noticed earlier says, "Excuse me young lady." (Young? Me? – I'm fifty-six!). He had seen the sign on my rucksack and wants to know all about it. While I satisfy my hunger, he goes round the regulars in the bar and collects twenty-eight pounds for me. Then he buys me a drink and I spend a pleasant evening in his company. He tells me that his father was a sailor and he was brought up by his gran. He was in the Army until an accident left him disabled.

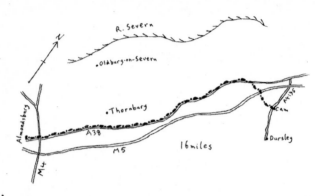

The hotel can't supply breakfast this morning, so after some bread and cheese I am on my way. It is a lovely bright morning with clear views of the Severn bridges – what a change from yesterday. Not all of today's route is on my maps, because I had intended to be further west than this. The A38 should get me to Dursley alright. It is a good road to walk along because it has a footpath alongside, separated from the road by a grass verge. I reckon I'll only need to follow my nose for about four miles, where my maps don't cover it.

It's a fairly uneventful day. The road takes me through Alveston, and into Gloucestershire at Stone. I go into a pub at lunchtime – nobody speaks to me except to take my order. The barmaid says "What can I get you sir?" then apologises when she realises her mistake.

When walking along roads, I am disgusted by the amount of litter I see in the hedgerows. Most of it is food-related – plastic bottles, drink cartons, crisp packets and such like. But I am amazed by the number of items of footwear, never a pair – a wellington boot, a child's trainer, a bright pink high-heeled shoe. Also workers' protective gloves, sometimes singly, sometimes with yards separating the pair.

I am back on the map as I approach my destination. Dursley is over to my right and there is a big black storm cloud above it. It starts to rain but only slightly – I am just on the edge of the storm. A bridge crosses the M5 motorway – it's fascinating to watch all these people who seem to be in such a hurry to get somewhere. The rain stops before I reach the guest house at Cam, where the landlady tells me they had a horrendous hailstorm.

After my bath, in the en suite bathroom with underfloor heating, I head for the nearest chip shop.

CHAPTER FIVE

You've got to have a dream
*If you don't have a dream,
How're you going to have a dream come true?*

In October 2001, Brian had an accident. He simply fell while exercising the dogs and tore a tendon in his knee. It had to be stitched back together, and he was in plaster for two months then more or less out of action for a further four months. This changed his attitude to life – now he says that you have to do what you want to do while you still can, because you don't know what's round the corner.

As a result of this, the following year we had a fantastic holiday in Canada, because he has always had a dream of going there. We took our granddaughter, who had her ninth birthday while we were there. We were enraptured by the amazing colours of the fall, and became almost addicted to pancakes with maple syrup.

Later he was planning a trip to Poland to shoot wild boar – an adventure I had no desire to accompany him on. We were discussing this one evening, so I asked him "Are you going to come with me when I walk from Land's End to John O'Groats?"

"No".

"I didn't think you would." (He couldn't do it anyway, the state his knees are in.)

He knew I had this dream as we'd talked about it before, but I don't think he'd realised how serious I was. We discussed it. I told him about my planned route and how I intended to organise accommodation. When he realised that I really wanted to do it he said "I'll have to get a Swedish au pair to take your place." (We were in bed at the time.)

"I don't know if it will ever happen – it's just something I want to do."

"Well do it then."

Any dream will do.

He's meeting me tonight in Gloucester.

Sunday 14/3/2004 Week 3

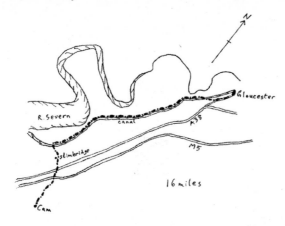

My landlady gives me a reduction on my bill and offers me
a lift to the Slimbridge roundabout. That would be acceptable if I
had come in from there last night, but it's in the opposite
direction, so it would be cheating. It's raining slightly as I head
down the road to the pretty village of Slimbridge, and onto the
towpath of the Gloucester and Sharpness Canal. This is a fine
wide canal completed in 1827 to allow ships to get up to
Gloucester more easily than via the nearby river Severn,
bypassing a dangerous stretch.

Between the canal and the river at Slimbridge is the
headquarters of the Wildfowl and Wetlands Trust, founded by
Sir Peter Scott in 1946 to conserve the environment for
migrating water birds.

The weather gets much wetter and windier, and I have to
put on my waterproof trousers for the first time. The wind is so
strong that it's making white horses on the canal, but at least it's
behind me, helping me along. My phone rings – it's my son
phoning to wish me a happy Mother's Day. "Thank you, son, but
I think that's next week!" At least he's thinking about me. I have
a chat with my granddaughter as well.

The original bridges over the canal were wooden, needing
two men to operate them for ships to go through, one a crew

member, the other a bridgeman who lived in a classical-style house near his bridge. The houses are now privately owned, and the bridges, now steel, can be operated by one man.

At Saul is the junction with the Stroudwater Navigation, which is undergoing restoration. This is a well-maintained area with canal-side facilities.

The towpath is a pleasant walk and the rain clears about lunchtime. The pretty yellow flowers of coltsfoot are growing all along the path. Brian phones – he's arrived in Gloucester and is looking for the hotel that I've booked. A pub beside the canal looks like a good place for lunch, but when I check the menu I decide it is far too dear. I just buy a drink and use the toilet, then return to the towpath and raid the supplies in my rucksack.

Between here and Gloucester there is a rowing regatta taking place on the canal – I bet they're glad that the weather has improved.

Brian is waiting for me when I arrive at the hotel soon after four o'clock. He is recovering well from the knee surgery, and can drive alright, though one of the wounds is weeping slightly. He has fetched my spare pair of boots, some clean clothes, and the rest of my maps, and will take home the maps I've finished with, some dirty washing and my other boots to clean and re-proof. When I've had a bath and relaxed for a while we go out for an excellent meal, then have a look at the docks in the dark. An information board tells us about a nine mile tramline that used to run to the docks, using horse drawn trucks – when they put a steam engine on it, it broke the rails.

Monday 15/3/2004

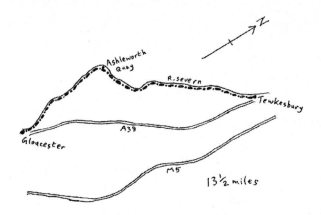

After a leisurely breakfast and more photos, we go our separate ways. When I signed the book at Land's End I was given a form to be stamped at Post Offices along the route, as evidence that I had done the walk – somehow I managed to leave it in the car. I have it now, so after a quick look at the cathedral I go in search of a Post Office. The clerk has never seen one of these forms before, but he obligingly stamps it.

Today's route follows the Severn Way all the way to Tewkesbury. It follows the riverbank fairly closely and is mostly a pleasant footpath. Shortly after leaving Gloucester I cross a wooden footbridge with the words 'THIS PATH IS ON PRAVITE [sic] LAND' painted in white on the planks. The land may be private but the general public have a right-of-way over it, though the dogs I meet don't seem to think so. The four black Labradors are far more aggressive than Labradors usually are. The youngest one starts to go for my leg, so I shout and wave my stick at it, and am relieved when they all run away.

At Ashleworth Quay there used to be a ferry across the river. The ferryman was also the landlord of The Boat public house on the other side.

Near Bishop's Norton the riverbank is very steep, so the

63

path leaves it and heads uphill through a wood. It is very muddy and slippery, and I am grateful for the handrail that has been provided. A nearby pub provides lunches – unfortunately it is shut on Mondays, so I feel justified in using the picnic benches outside, which are for customers' use only, according to a large sign.

On checking my phone I find that Mary has left a voice-mail (probably while I was dealing with the dogs). There's no point me phoning her back as she's out this afternoon – she'll probably phone again the minute I arrive at tonight's guest house.

There's lots of pussy willow in this area, and signs saying 'No elvering' – well it makes a change from 'No fishing'! The path now follows a man-made embankment close to the river. A line of debris near the top of the embankment, sometimes over the top, shows where the floods came to a few weeks ago. I wouldn't have been able to walk on this path then. Most of the debris is decaying vegetation – rushes, twigs, etc, but there is also a lot of litter, mostly plastic bottles. My eye is drawn to a yellow plastic duck.

Just before five o'clock I arrive at the guest house in Tewkesbury, where the landlord asks me to leave my boots in the hall (they are very muddy today). Just as I'm taking them off, Mary phones again (what did I tell you?), so when I'm settled into my room I phone her back and make arrangements for meeting tomorrow. I need more groceries so I go and do some shopping, and have a meal in a burger bar. My daughter phones while I'm eating and we have a chat. Later I phone my mother – she's happier when I tell her that my knees aren't aching so much now, but she still hasn't got confidence in my ability to complete the walk. I'll show her!

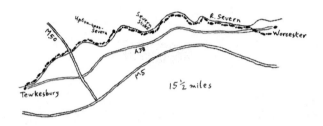

When I get up, it looks like it's going to be a wet day, but the clouds soon vanish and it turns into a lovely sunny day. I am following the Severn Way again today, on the west bank of the river now; it was on the east bank previously. It's nice and level with a few stiles, which I can manage a lot more easily now that my knees are better. I must be fitter than I've ever been in my life.

As I approach the M50 motorway, that crosses the river on a viaduct, a light aircraft flies low overhead. Has Brian hired it to spy on me and take photos? No, probably not! Yesterday it was low-flying military planes – I can't get away from them. The traffic in the nearside lane of the motorway has stopped, and I wonder why. Then I see that the car in front is a police car and a policeman is getting out. He removes some rubbish (it looks like a piece of tyre) from the carriageway and they all get going again. I can't get my camera out quickly enough to capture it on film, so I take a snap of an Eddie Stobbart lorry instead.

Mary phones to see how far I've got. She's coming on the bus to Severn Stoke and will meet me near there at lunch time. Soon I am approaching Upton-upon-Severn, which is bordered by a large grassy meadow in a bend of the river. There is evidence that the meadow has been flooded recently; the remains of many leaves are lying about, the flesh of each leaf rotted away leaving only a skeleton of veins. I pick one up, and it isn't as fragile as I thought it would be, in fact it's quite robust, so I pack it away between two maps.

Upton-upon-Severn is a pleasant little town, with gift shops, boats on the river, and a Heritage Centre with a memorial to Sir William Tennant. This gentleman achieved fame in the Second World War when he spearheaded the operation to evacuate the beaches of Dunkirk. He also played a large part in the success of the D-Day landings, commanding the installation of the floating Mulberry harbours and the laying of the fuel pipeline across the Channel. (You have probably realised by now that all these bits of background information are being added later, mostly gleaned from the Internet, while writing this book – I'm zooming through the country too fast to absorb it all during the Walk.)

When I was planning the walk, I wrote to all the Tourist Information Centres along the route, requesting information about accommodation, etc. The response from Upton-upon-Severn was excellent, so I pop into the office to thank them and have a chat. They wish me luck and I continue on my way, crossing back to the east bank of the river.

Just south of Severn Stoke, the Severn Way leaves the riverbank to avoid some private property, and it is here that I meet Mary. Even though I like walking on my own, it's nice to have company for a change, and it's useful to be with someone who knows the area. At this point the Way doubles back on itself round the other side of the private land and back to the river, but it's simpler just to follow a track into Severn Stoke. Here we sit on a bench by the war memorial to eat our lunch and get to know each other. We find we have a lot in common, including similar thermal cushions! She tells me about a lady she met on the bus, who left her handbag on it and had to wait for the bus to return from Upton-upon-Severn so that she could get it back.

After lunch we rejoin the Severn Way at the riverbank, but soon it cuts across fields. We see a huge conveyor belt carrying gravel from a quarry to goodness knows where. Close by is a large patch of wild flowers – red dead-nettle and the sky-blue flowers of speedwell. Further on the Way goes back to the river, but it is blocked by debris from the floods, so we have to find our way across the fields. Mary's large-scale map comes in useful here. Another walker catches us up, so we exchange a few words with him, and also have a chat to a groundsman working at a boat club.

Across the fields we can see the Severn Trow House, a pub at Kempsey. The trow was a flat-bottomed wooden sailing ship, only used on the Severn, and now used as a logo for the Severn Way.

Mary guides me to her house on the southern side of Worcester, feeds me an excellent meal, and we spend the evening in pleasant conversation. Last weekend she was staying in Rochester, Kent, where she was born and bred. The B&B where she stayed is next door but one to my uncle's house. It's a small world!

* W e d n e s d a y   1 7 / 3 / 2 0 0 4 *

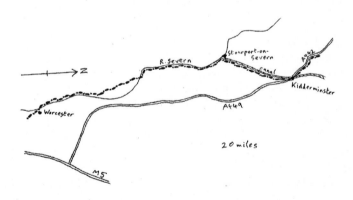

Mary has a clock on her kitchen wall. At first glance it's a normal, plain, round clock, but you look at it to check the time, and you think it must be wrong. Then you notice that the numbers are arranged anticlockwise and you realise that the hands are also going anticlockwise, and the time is actually right. It's very confusing until you get used to it.

We have scrambled eggs and mushrooms for breakfast, and

Mary accompanies me through the town centre. It feels strange not having to check the map every step of the way – towns are harder to navigate through than countryside, unless you have a street plan. We pass the Cathedral and close by, an old church spire with no church attached to it. It is the remains of St Andrews, demolished in 1949 leaving just the tower and spire, known locally as the 'Glover's Needle' – Worcester was a major glove-making centre. It certainly looks like a needle; the open arches at the bottom forming the eye.

Near the footbridge over the river we have arranged to meet a friend from the local hospice and a photographer from the local newspaper. It's nice to get a bit of publicity – I don't suppose it will result in any sponsorship money for me, but at least it might raise awareness of the hospice. We duly have our photographs taken and continue on our way. Mary comes with me as far as the City boundary, where we say goodbye and promise to keep in touch. Soon afterwards, the path goes through an arboretum, with an inscription on the gate.

Walk on a rainbow trail,
Walk on a trail of song,
And all about you will be beauty,
There is a way out of every dark mist over a rainbow trail.

In places, the river Severn splits, with half going over a weir, and half going through a lock, to keep the river navigable. I never knew that. It's amazing what you learn! I spot a sign on the opposite side of the river that says 'Droitwich canal restoration for Mid-Worcs Ring'. A major canal restoration project is being undertaken in the area – it's good to see so many canals being restored in different parts of the country.

There are a lot of wood anemones in this area – a pretty white star-shaped flower, sometimes known as windflower. The Severn Way leaves the river again and goes through the village of Grimley, before passing straight through the middle of a quarry. There are signs everywhere to make sure you stay on the designated path. Then I come to the bridge over the river at Holt. This is currently closed to traffic – Mary knew about this and had phoned to make sure that it was open to pedestrians. She had actually spoken to the foreman. Consequently, the workmen, who are having a break when I arrive are expecting me and greet me with "You made it then!", then joke about what would I do if they said I couldn't cross the bridge.

On a track through a wooded area, I sit on a pile of pallets to eat my lunch. A group of about twenty walkers pass by, hardly glancing at me – this is most unusual as fellow walkers normally exchange a cheery 'Hello'. The path is pleasant to walk on, apart from a rough bit just south of Stourport-on-Severn. On the other side of the river are some interesting-looking caves cut into the red sandstone. These were a hermitage for hundreds of years, occupied for a time by about a hundred monks.

At Stourport-on-Severn a flight of locks connects the river to the Staffordshire and Worcestershire canal. Stourport Basins, once full of working barges, are a picturesque sight with the many brightly-coloured leisure craft.

After searching for a shop to buy a drink, I join the towpath and have a pleasant walk to Kidderminster. On the outskirts of the town I meet two young girls on bikes, who ask me lots of questions about what I'm doing. "Don't you get scared?" one of them asks, her mouth full of banana.

I leave the canal in the town so that I can get to my B&B by the shortest possible route. I spot an estate agent's office with the name 'Doolittle & Dalley'! Mary used to live in this area, and she told me about a handy supermarket on the way, so I stock up here and continue to the farm cottage just outside town. On the way I see a sign 'TELFORD 25 miles'. I work in Telford, so I'm quite close to my office desk. Aarrgghh!!

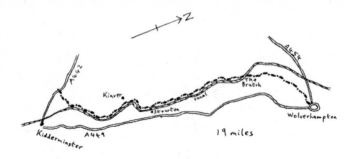

This morning I have to retrace my steps for a mile before rejoining the canal at Wolverley. Here I get confused and nearly follow the bank of the river Stour instead of the canal towpath, but I soon discover my mistake. It's canal most of the way today, still the Staffordshire and Worcestershire. When I reach Stourton, my daughter phones to see how I'm getting on – I'm staying at her home in Wolverhampton tonight.

At Stourton there is a junction with the Stourbridge canal. I watch a barge come down the main canal, do a three-point turn in the junction, and head back up. Later, I am sitting by a lock eating my lunch, when the same barge comes through. A lady jumps off to operate the lock, but goes to the wrong end and starts to fill it instead of emptying it – the water level has to be the same as the outside level before the boat can enter and rise through the lock. She corrects herself and they go on their way.

There are some interesting things to see beside the canal. At the Staffordshire/Worcestershire border (that I passed this morning) a fine stone marks the border. On the other side of the canal, north of Stourton, is a cave known as Devil's Den, which I believe is a boathouse carved into the cliff. I also see something that looks like a dog kennel, but it is at the edge of the water and there is a large egg close to the entrance, so I decide it must be a duck kennel. And today's flower is a pink spike that I think is bistort.

When I get to the flight of locks at The Bratch, it starts to rain quite heavily – it was raining first thing this morning but cleared up before lunchtime. Here I leave the canal and join an old railway line that has been converted to a cycle track. I follow this for three miles to Castlecroft, then two miles of streets to my daughter's house in the high-rise flats close to Wolverhampton's ring road. I notice a familiar car parked in the street, and when Maria answers the intercom, I say "What's he doing here?" It's Brian of course, come for his tea because it's not too far from home. I have a nice relaxing evening, taking time to cuddle my granddaughter who is nearly three months old now. She's grown a lot since I last saw her.

Friday 19/3/2004

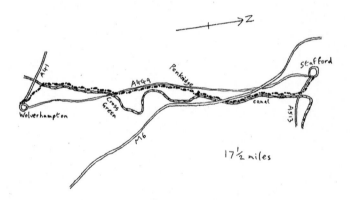

I boil myself some eggs for breakfast. Maria isn't up yet; she has to get her rest whenever she can, as the baby doesn't sleep all night. They appear while I'm eating, so I've got time for a chat and a cuddle before I get on my way. It's drizzling so I put on my waterproof jacket, but don't bother with the trousers.

A pleasant walk across the park takes me to a small shopping centre, where I go in the Post Office to get my form stamped and buy two Mother's Day cards – one for my mother and one for my mother-in-law. When I come out it is absolutely bucketing down. I consider that such a heavy shower can't possibly last very long, but it continues for about half an hour as I walk through the streets towards the canal. The gutters are rivers and my trousers are soaked.

I join the canal near the racecourse. The rain is slackening now, and it stops by the time I reach Aldersley Junction. Here the Wolverhampton Locks, a flight of twenty-one, lead to the Birmingham canal. Unfortunately all I can see is the bottom gates of the first lock, because I'm on the other side of the canal (still the Staffs & Worcs). Now that the rain has stopped my trousers dry out remarkably quickly.

My regular Friday phone call from Mike comes at an 'inconvenient' moment – I am behind a hedge with my pants down! While we're on the subject, it's surprising how easy it is to find somewhere to 'go'. In country areas there are not many people about, and you can usually get into a field and hide behind a hedge. In towns there are pubs, cafes and filling stations. The only trouble is that you tend to be thinking about it more and looking for good places – consequently the need arises more often.

The canal meanders about quite a lot between here and Penkridge, so I leave it at Cross Green and walk up the main road, the A449, instead. It has a fine footpath and is not unpleasant, and I reckon it will save me a couple of miles. Beyond Penkridge the canal is straighter, so I rejoin it and follow it towards Stafford. Canals are normally quiet, peaceful places, but the tranquillity is spoilt here by the constant rumble of traffic on the nearby M6.

Two miles of city streets take me to tonight's guest house near the town centre. There is a very nice theatre in Stafford, which I have visited on previous occasions, so I decide to check whether anything is on tonight. Unfortunately there isn't, so I look for somewhere to eat, and have scampi and chips in a pleasant restaurant.

CHAPTER SIX

Somewhere, over the rainbow
Skies are blue,
And the dreams that you dare to dream
Really do come true

Rainbows are wonderful phenomena. I love them.

I've mentioned that I work in Telford but live in Mid-Wales. It's more than fifty miles, which is a long drive each day, especially as a lot of it is country lanes, so normally I commute weekly, renting a room in a shared house a short walk from the office. This all changed when Brian had his accident, however. He could manage to look after himself, but he couldn't exercise the dogs or muck out the pony. This meant that for six months I had to get up early to see to the animals before getting changed and driving to work, then after a full day's work I didn't get home until seven o'clock, and all I wanted to do after a meal was fall asleep in front of the telly. As you can imagine, it was very tiring, the worst part of it being that there was no time for *me*.

One morning it was raining while I was doing my chores, which was depressing, but as soon as I got in the car to drive to work, it started to ease off – 'Typical!' I thought. The sun broke through, and as I turned onto the main road, there right in front of me was the most magnificent rainbow I've ever seen in my life, its brilliant colours set against a black sky. 'Ah, that's just for me', I thought, and in a literal sense it was, because the rainbow that you see is not the same one that I see, even if you are standing next to me. I really felt that it had been specially arranged just for me, and it lifted my spirits.

Then there was the time, during my rambling days in Scotland, when I was leading a walk in the Ballater area. As we started off along the south side of the river Dee, there was a fine rainbow on the north side. I commented that it was exactly where we would be later on. Annabel asked "Do you think we'll find a pot of gold?".

"We always find a pot of gold, don't we Annabel?" I replied.

"Yes, we do," she said – she knew exactly what I meant. I was of course referring to the happiness gained from walking in the fresh air, in beautiful surroundings, with pleasant companions.

I believe I've mentioned Jimmy Logan's charity concert? The night it took place I was at the cinema. I knew the concert was planned, but didn't know when it was going to be, and I wouldn't have been able to get up to Glasgow for it anyway. The film was 'Finding Forrester' starring Sean Connery. It is about a reclusive author who is brought out of his shell by a young student, but in the end he goes back to his native Scotland and dies of cancer. This naturally struck a chord with me, knowing how ill my idol was, and as I came out of the cinema I couldn't stop the tears flowing. I wondered later whether I'd picked up some of the emotional vibes from the concert, which I didn't know was taking place at that very moment. I think the tears were partly for me, though – I suddenly felt that I didn't have a goal in life and that I'd lived half a century without doing anything really useful. This was partly triggered by the words of 'Somewhere, over the rainbow', which was used as a theme song for the film I had just seen. I knew I had to *do* something, and that something was, of course, the Walk that I am now in the middle of.

If happy little bluebirds fly
Beyond the rainbow, why oh why can't I?

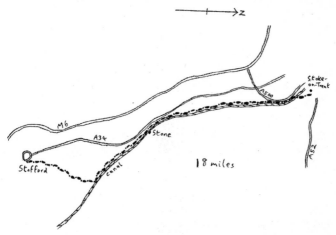

My landlady is quite talkative this morning; she wants to know all about my walk. She wants to give me a £5 donation but hasn't got anything smaller than a £20 note. I manage to produce £13.50 in change, and she says, "That'll do." I tell her about Brian's accident, and we talk about life, and how it should be lived to the full. She has a friend in San Francisco who used to buy a piece of china every time she came to England, but it was all broken in the earthquake, so she doesn't buy any more now because it no longer matters. Life is more important.

I head northwards out of town, and join the canal near Sandon – a different one now, the Trent and Mersey. Two men are working on a boat – they see the sign on my rucksack and wish me luck. The weather is overcast today, there's a heavy shower, then it becomes very windy. A couple are feeding ducks on the towpath and we pass the time of day. The man asks me what factor sun cream I'm using. I know he's only joking, but the fact is that I always use a moisturiser with sun protection.

Stone looks like a pleasant, busy sort of town, but I don't have time to go and explore it. A lot of people are taking exercise on the towpath. A man living on a boat strikes up a conversation – he used to live in Cornwall and says he has done a lot of walking. He invites me in for a drink, but I decline as I have to get on my way.

At Meaford Locks I stop for lunch and watch three boats coming down through the flight. They appear to be all together. A middle-aged lady disembarks with a toddler in a lifejacket and they explore the area between the lock gates. A couple decide to walk down as far as the next lock, and ask me how far it is. A man on the third boat, who says they are all trying to get to a pub in Stone in time for the Rugby match, gives me a donation of £10.

A bridge over the canal has the word 'SMILE' painted on it, with a smiley face underneath. It makes me laugh and I decide that not all graffiti is bad.

The wind has been getting steadily worse all day. An old man tells me that there is a tree down, further up the canal. When I get there it is quite a sight. The tree is straight across the canal like a bridge, blocking it completely. The branches at the top have demolished a garden shed on the other side. As I continue on my way, I shout a warning to boats on their way down. Soon I come to a straight bit of canal where there used to be collieries in the area. It is very open here – there is no shelter from the wind at all, so I keep well away from the water's edge, for fear of being blown in.

Before long I am in Stoke-on-Trent, 'The Potteries', where names such as Wedgewood, Minton, Spode and Twyford found fame. Once there were dozens of the bottle-shaped kilns, but very few remain now, and the city is trying to re-invent itself; I'm not sure what as.

Part of the towpath in Stoke-on-Trent is closed, but only for a short distance, so I soon get round the diversion back on to the towpath. As I'm checking the map to find the best way to the guest house, a man greets me with "There's only one way you *can* go!" (this is certainly true on a towpath).

After finding the guest house near the bus station, I go back down the road to the chip shop. When I get back, there is a phone call from Ann, another rambler, who will be putting me up in Buxton the day after tomorrow.

*

Since joining the canals three days ago, I have seen boats of all shapes and sizes, from working barges (not many of these nowadays) to holiday narrowboats to motor cruisers, but all of course narrow enough to negotiate the many locks on the canal system. It is interesting to note some of the names that people have given to their boats. A boatyard in Stone has many narrowboats, all with a similar design, and all with girls' names, including Katherine and Maria. Presumably these boats will be exploring the canals once the holiday season gets under way. Other names I have spotted are Inaminit, Dunitagen, Hagar, Omega, Fortuitous, Strait & Narrow, Silent Swan, Tigger (which was towing another boat), Mr Mole Too, and Sovereign.

Sunday 21/3/2004 Week 4

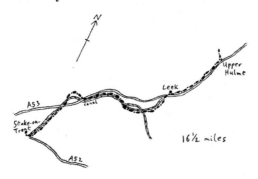

Breakfast is quite a leisurely affair – there appears to be only one cook/waitress and she has a lot of guests to serve, so it takes a while. A notice tells guests to sit at the table corresponding to their room number, but I can't see any numbers on the tables – they must be invisible numbers because the cook moves some people to their correct tables. The couple on the next table are quite talkative. They have been visiting the theatre and making a weekend of it. I tell them about my Adventure and they wish me luck.

After phoning my mother to wish her a happy Mother's Day (or Mothering Sunday, as she prefers to call it), I wander round the town centre for ages, looking for somewhere to buy drinks and chocolate. I know it's Sunday, but you'd think there would be a newsagent or something open. Eventually the Iceland supermarket opens at ten o'clock, and I am able to stock up.

The Trent & Mersey canal continues in a north-westerly direction, but I am going north-east, along the Caldon canal. A road within the town crosses the canal by an interesting lift bridge, electrically operated when boats want to go through.

Near Milton a large sign proclaims that the towpath is closed. This is obviously for re-surfacing work – there is work in progress, though not today of course, it being Sunday. There is no indication of how far it is closed for, nor what route is advised for diversion. I decide to ignore the sign and carry on along the half-made towpath, but soon my way is blocked by a high wire fence, and I have to find my own diversion along roads, rejoining the canal at Stockton Brook. It's just as well I've got decent maps.

My son phones to wish me a happy Mother's Day (again!). As we talk I lean on the parapet of a bridge over the entrance to the boatyard of Stoke-on-Trent Boat Club. This is Endon Basin, which was once an interchange basin between the canal and the railway. The railway is now disused.

At Hazlehurst Locks the canal splits. The main Caldon branch forks left, goes down through the locks, and eventually heads south. The Leek branch forks right, then turns left, crossing the Caldon branch over an aqueduct before heading northwards towards Leek. This seems to me to be a curious arrangement, but I suppose there must have been a good reason for it at the time. In this area I spot some more unusual boat names, such as Moonlight, Half Past Four, Bubbles On The Water, Felix, Witch Way, and Mum's Folly. The latter makes me ponder – is it a folly, this Endeavour that I have embarked upon?

The Leek branch passes through some very pleasant

countryside. About a mile before Leek it goes through a 130 yard tunnel, where the towpath leaves the canal and climbs over the hill. The bargemen of old would have had to 'leg' the barge through the tunnel, while a younger member of the family led the horse over the hill. The canal only continues for about a mile beyond the tunnel, finishing at an aqueduct over the river Churnet. The last half mile from here to Leek Basin has been filled in.

Leek is sometimes described as the 'Queen of the Moorlands', surrounded as it is by beautiful scenery. There used to be a thriving silk industry here but of course this has declined, as have traditional industries everywhere – it's a great shame.

As I arrive in Leek, I am greeted by a tremendous thunderclap directly overhead, and the heavens open – rain, hail, the lot, and I'm soaked in no time. I have my waterproof jacket on, but not the trousers. I had intended to get something to eat in the town, but I don't fancy going into a cafe in this half-drowned state, so I press on towards Upper Hulme. The rain stops and I begin to dry out, but then it starts again. A man in a yellow pick-up truck stops and offers me a lift – "No thanks, I'm nearly there." It's too wet to linger and explain that it would be cheating. When I get to the farmhouse B&B I strip off and spread everything out to dry. My rucksack has a waterproof cover, but some dampness still manages to get in. The clothes are in a plastic bag and are okay, but I spread the rest of the contents over the floor. I'm just coming out of the shower when my daughter phones to wish me a happy Mother's Day.

Monday 22/3/2004

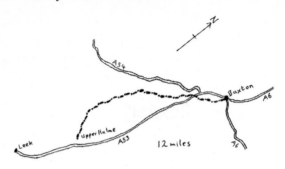

After a fine breakfast and a reduction in the bill, I repack my gear and get ready to go. The weather forecast is quite bad today, and I don't want another soaking like yesterday, so I get myself fully kitted out with waterproof jacket and trousers. Actually it turns out mostly sunny but blustery with a few wintry showers. The over-trousers keep my trousers clean and help to keep me warm.

There is a footpath following the ridge of the Roaches, but I decide it will be simpler to stay on the road which runs parallel to the hills as far as Roach End, where I take a path through Back Forest to Gradbach. Ann tells me later that there used to be wallabies living wild in this area – presumably escapees.

Now I follow the Dane Valley Way towards Three Shire Heads, at which point the counties of Cheshire, Staffordshire and Derbyshire meet. Unfortunately I take the wrong path at a fork and miss it, so I don't manage to step into Cheshire at all, though I'm soon in Derbyshire.

My route now is partly easy tracks and partly boggy footpaths. I discover I have a voice-mail from James, my team leader at work – he must have phoned when I had no signal. I phone him back and tell him how much I'm enjoying myself. It's really great now that my legs have stopped aching. As I approach Buxton across Axe Edge Moor, I am met by a hail storm that stings my face, but it doesn't last long.

80

I drop down into the town via Grinlow quarry, which has been transformed into a pleasant Country Park – on a hill to my right is the folly of Solomon's Temple. After getting my form stamped and buying some groceries, I find my way to Ann's house. She and her husband have been to his mother's funeral today, but they still give me a warm welcome. They don't have a TV, but Ann keeps me entertained with tales of their many walking holidays in France and Spain.

Tuesday 23/3/2004

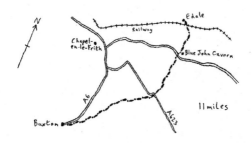

We have sausages for breakfast, and Ann accompanies me on the first part of today's walk. We cross the golf course on Fairfield Common and follow footpaths to Peak Dale. On a path overlooking a railway line we meet a friend of hers walking her dog, so we stop for a chat. Later we find that some of the public footpaths are difficult to follow, and find ourselves on a farm track, that we are told, in no uncertain terms, is private. We apologise and are directed to the correct path.

We soon join the Limestone Way, a long distance path that runs for fifty miles between Rocester in Staffordshire and Castleton in Derbyshire. Here Ann has to leave me to go back home, and I continue alone up the Limestone Way. This section is uphill, and is badly rutted, presumably by the irresponsible use of off-road motorbikes. I leave the Way and follow a long straight track with a good view of the hill of Mam Tor ahead.

A road takes me to the Blue John Cavern, where I decide that I have time for a tour of the caves. They won't take me on my own, so I have to wait until a young couple arrive and they can take the three of us. There are a lot of steps to climb down (and up again), but it is all very impressive. The Blue John stone is very pretty – the name comes from the French 'bleu jaune' meaning 'blue yellow', and these are the colours of the stone. I buy a small one as a souvenir.

Along the base of Mam Tor runs a road which curves back in a loop towards Castleton. Or rather, I should say, it used to run. A lengthy section of the road was the victim of subsidence many years ago, and was closed to traffic in 1979. It is fascinating to see the surviving sections of tarmac, complete with white lines, but all at different levels. It is still passable on foot, though some of the drops between levels are so steep that it is better to stay on the grass above the road.

From the top of the loop, a steep path climbs a ridge to Hollins Cross. Here a whole new vista suddenly opens up. This is the heart of the Peak District – below me is a wide valley with the village of Edale, tonight's destination, nestling at the bottom. Beyond is Kinder Scout, which I intend to climb tomorrow.

I descend steeply into the valley, and arrive at my B&B next to the church in Edale at 4:30 to find a note pinned to the door – 'Back at 5pm'. I take the opportunity to explore the village, and have a look at the church, which is not locked. There is a box for donations to save the spire, so I relieve my purse of some loose change.

The B&B is a lovely old house, with a very old-fashioned, but perfectly functional bathroom. On a chest of drawers on the landing is a basket, containing a selection of maps and guide books for the use of guests. After a soak in the beautiful cast-iron bath, I go down the road to the pub for a baked potato, which I request without salad, but it arrives with – there is also onion in the tuna, which wasn't specified on the menu. Yes, I know, I'm a fussy so-and-so, but I do wish people could do what you ask, and make things clearer on menus.

Kath signing the book of End-to-Enders at Land's End

Chun Quoit – Iron Age burial cairn in Cornwall

I

The Somerset Levels – nearly sunset with the old windmill mocking me in the distance.

Magnolia bush in Carlisle

II

Good Friday – Walk of Witness in Milngavie

Signing the book of End-to Enders at John O' Groats, with husband Brian

Fallen tree blocking the Trent & Mersey canal near Stoke

Nature's sculptures on Kinder Scout

Dent Dale Cumbria

Loch Lomond from the north

Ben Nevis with fresh snow, seen from Loch Lochy

**First glimpse of the northern coast and the
Island of Stroma- nearly there!**

Fallen tree blocking the Trent & Mersey canal near Stoke

Nature's sculptures on Kinder Scout

Dent Dale Cumbria

Loch Lomond from the north

Ben Nevis with fresh snow, seen from Loch Lochy

**First glimpse of the northern coast and the
Island of Stroma- nearly there!**

CHAPTER SEVEN

Climb every mountain
Ford every stream,
Follow every rainbow
Till you find your dream

* W e d n e s d a y   24/3/2004 *

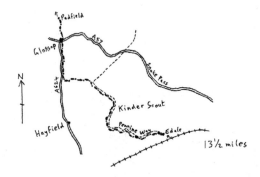

My landlord is selling some home-made 'granny's flapjack' in aid of the church spire. It looks delicious, so I buy some. Then I don my waterproofs as it is raining slightly, and it will probably be quite cold up in the hills.

The Pennine Way was first suggested in 1935, in an article in the *Daily Herald* by the late Tom Stephenson, who was the Ramblers' Association secretary for many years. The National Trail starts in Edale, but I shan't be following all of it, just bits wherever it suits me.

In the village I follow the signpost with its acorn symbol, used for all National Trails in England and Wales. This takes me down an alleyway and a sheltered path beside a stream, then a stile leads to a path across fields to Upper Booth. I know that much of the Way has been paved because of the erosion caused by thousands of walking boots, and these fields are no exception – stone slabs are laid along the path like stepping-stones. Near Upper Booth is a barn containing information about the Way, and paintings done by local schoolchildren. Soon afterwards, I come to the steep footpath known as Jacob's Ladder. This climbs in a zigzag, set with stones all the way up. I can see that today is going to be the hardest yet, but at least I've built up my fitness now, so it shouldn't be a problem.

After some more climbing, where I am overtaken by some other walkers, I eventually reach the summit of Kinder Low, on the edge of the upland gritstone plateau of Kinder Scout. This is where the famous mass trespass took place in 1932. The land was private and walkers were not allowed, so hundreds of ramblers congregated to stage a (hopefully) peaceful protest. There were scuffles with gamekeepers and six of the trespassers were arrested, but their actions paved the way for the opening up of the countryside, so that future generations could enjoy the hills.

It's a different world up here. Although the climbing is over, the terrain can hardly be described as flat. Black mounds of soft peat, like giant sponges, known as haggs, are interspersed with lower patches of rough grass and wet, reedy areas, or groughs. The path disappears among this chaotic landscape, and I'm glad it's not foggy – in fact the weather is mostly fine with a few wintry showers, as good as can be expected at this time of year.

One of the walkers has a GPS exactly the same as mine. It is certainly useful for checking your position, though all you really need to do is stay within sight of the edge, where the ground falls away steeply, and just keep going round the edge of the plateau. Picking your way among the haggs and groughs is quite difficult, but the most confusing thing is that the miles are longer up here, or so it seems.

The path starts to re-appear as I approach Kinder Downfall, where the water from the plateau cascades over the edge, eventually to be captured in Kinder Reservoir. The landscape is more rocky now; I've left the black peat behind. The wind and rain of ages have created some fascinating sculptures beside the path, which continues along the edge of the plateau. At last I leave the heights and drop down steeply to the top of William Clough, a deep ravine which takes more water to the reservoir. Then, at the top of Mill Hill, the Pennine Way turns right, but I part company with it and follow a path straight ahead in a nice steady descent over Burnt Hill. Much of this path is paved with slabs of stone, which is probably just as well, as the surrounding ground is very boggy. It leads me to a main road about three miles south of Glossop.

Although it has been a strenuous day today, I'm really glad that I decided to include this bit of mountaineering in my Adventure. It's the most amazing place, especially with its history, and I'll never forget it.

Okay, so it's back to mundane roads now. In Glossop I do some shopping and call at the Post Office before finding my B&B at Padfield, where I have an excellent meal at the local pub.

I have some phone calls to make tonight, to book ahead again. Whenever I make a booking, I always mention that I'm walking from Land's End to John O'Groats. In five days time, I'll be in a place called Dent, near Sedbergh. I'm talking to the landlady there and she's really interested – she asks me where I'll be the night before Dent – "Horton-in-Ribblesdale."

"And where are you just now?"

"Er...er..." – it takes me a few moments to remember! It can be quite confusing sleeping in a different bed every night.

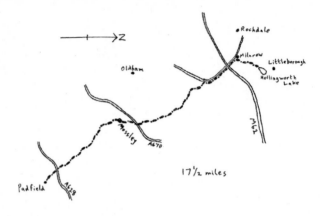

An early breakfast and a donation from the landlady, and I am on my way again. I soon cross a bridge over an old railway line converted to a cycle track. According to my brother, we once travelled on that railway in the 1950s. Then I go down through Hadfield and up through Tintwistle, where I have a bit of trouble finding the right road. The Tameside Trail takes me over the hill past the Swineshaw Reservoirs to Mossley.

The rest of today's walk is going to be very bitty, with a multitude of different possible routes across this sprawling area of mixed town and country. I'll just have to play it by ear. In Mossley I find a pleasant-looking footpath through a wooded area. It starts off alright, but is not very satisfactory – I end up having to climb a fence to get onto the road. Further on I misread the map and turn right before the railway station instead of after it. This of course means that I am on the wrong side of the railway line – I have gone nearly a mile before I realise my mistake, so I have to look for an alternative. I find a footpath that crosses the railway near Quick and this puts me back on course. I'm going to stick to roads the rest of the way today. That should keep it simple. What a contrast to yesterday's lofty heights!

I am in a fairly rural area now and the roads take me

through Lydgate, High Moor, and Grains Bar. On the way I am asked for directions twice – I can't help the delivery man who is looking for '405 Oldham Road', but I am able to give some rough directions to the motorist who wants Uppermill as it's on my map. I contemplate whether to use some footpath short cuts that are marked on the map, but they don't look very inviting so I leave them alone.

The road down Dog Hill has a sign – 'Snow – Road Closed When Lights Flash'. I haven't seen any snow since Bristol. The main road goes through Newhey, under the M62, and into Milnrow, where I go up through the side streets and past a fine church. A lorry with a crane on it is unloading a container over a wall with iron railings into the grounds of a school, presumably for an extra classroom. I stand and watch it for a few minutes.

What is this life, if, full of care,
We have no time to stand and stare?

Yes, I know that's meant for more sublime things than lorries unloading containers, but it's all part of life's rich tapestry.

A straight road goes up towards Littleborough. Brian is meeting me there tonight so I phone him – he's on his way. Maybe he'll get there before me. He could even pass me along this road. I arrive first and phone him again, then pass the phone to Chris, the landlady, so that she can give him precise directions, and he arrives about two minutes later. We have a beautiful room with an en suite shower room, which Chris says we can have for nothing, as I am doing the walk for charity. She also suggests that I might like to have a bath – I reply that I would love one; I always prefer to have a bath if I can, to soak the aching muscles after the day's walk. The communal bathroom has fully tiled walls; the door is tiled to match, and there's a full-length mirror beside it. As I lie soaking, I ponder that I wouldn't like to be drunk or half asleep in here as it would be hard to find the way out!

We round off the day with a meal at an excellent restaurant beside Hollingworth Lake.

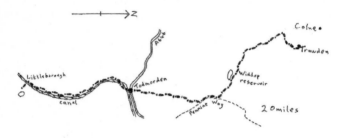

Brian asks Chris how much we owe her for his breakfast, but she absolutely refuses any payment. We say our goodbyes and I head off down the road and onto the towpath of the Rochdale Canal. Yes, another canal; they really are great for walking along.

A man with a dog catches me up – "You're not really walking all the way to John O'Groats are you?" We get into conversation and he tells me about the railway tunnel built by Stevenson, which runs parallel to the canal, where a petrol tanker went on fire some years ago. This was in 1984, when a train derailed and caught fire, sending a huge fireball through one of the ventilation shafts. Two-hundred people were evacuated and it was several days before the tunnel cooled down enough for the damage to be inspected.

Unknown to me, Brian is filming me from a bridge over the canal. He meets me on the towpath where it overlooks the start of the railway tunnel. After more photos and more goodbyes I continue alone again. The canal rises gradually through a series of locks to Summit, which is actually the name of a small village at the summit, then descends in the same manner. As I cross the border from Lancashire into Yorkshire my mobile rings – it's my usual weekly call from Mike.

At Todmorden the railway crosses the canal on an impressive viaduct. In the town I top up my mobile phone. Then I find my way up the hill through the side streets to Hale Bottom. I go astray a bit here, but there are plenty of paths and I soon get back onto my intended route, with the help of two transmitters which are good landmarks. Then a farm track to Four Gates End, and a public footpath which is not easy to follow. On the way to a farm called Egypt, I have my lunch sitting on the windowsill of a ruined farmhouse.

The Pennine Way keeps me company again, but only briefly – I leave it after a mile and head uphill on a narrow road past Widdop Reservoir. It is very bleak and windy up here. It's now country roads all the way, up and down and up and down, past Coldwell Reservoir, to my farmhouse B&B at Trawden, near Colne. The farmer's wife is very friendly, and gives me a glass of milk. The farmer offers to give me a lift to the pub to get a meal, but I decide I would rather just relax and raid my supplies. It's been a long day today. Twenty miles; the longest for over a week.

CHAPTER EIGHT

Daisies are our silver
Buttercups our gold,
This is all the treasure
We can have or hold

Saturday 27/3/2004

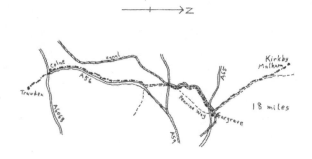

This is a lovely old farmhouse, with stone walls, wooden beams and mullioned windows. The farmer's wife tells me that when they moved in thirty years ago, it had been modernised in 1960s style, and it has been a labour of love to renovate it and fill it with beautiful old furniture. She gives me a donation and makes a packed lunch for me.

I follow a path across a field, then a country lane takes me down to a bridge over Colne Water and steeply up into the town of Colne, in Lancashire – I wasn't in Yorkshire very long yesterday. Here I do some shopping and buy a birthday card for my daughter.

While I am looking for a Post Office, I discover that there is an excellent market, but I find that I have no desire to browse round the stalls. It makes me think about the old children's hymn that is the heading for this chapter. It was always a favourite of mine, and I have always had the opinion that there are more important things than money. The world has become so commercial, with so many things offered for sale wherever you go, but very few are things that you actually *need*. As long as you have food, clothes, warmth and shelter, the rest is just desire rather than need. These feelings have been strengthened in me by doing this walk. My needs are simple. I wear the same clothes every day with very few spares in my rucksack, and as long as I can get a bed each night I am contented. Also I am in the fresh air every day, savouring the wonderful variety of our British countryside.

I find a Post Office along the road towards Earby. The clerk stamps my form and says "That's LE-JOG isn't it? – Are you going to JOG-LE back?" The A56 has a good footpath most of the way, and goes straight up through Earby. On the way a young couple in a car stop and give me a handful of loose change – it adds up to £3.45.

At Thornton-in-Craven I leave the road and rejoin my old friend the Pennine Way, as it ambles up a lane and across a field onto the towpath of yet another canal, the Leeds and Liverpool. I'm in Yorkshire again. At East Marton an interesting double bridge crosses the canal – apparently the second arch was built on top of the first to eliminate a dip in the road. Soon after this the Pennine Way leaves the canal and heads in a fairly straight line to Gargrave. I decide to stay with the canal, even though it meanders a bit, with large zigzags round the contours of the landscape. At least it's nice level walking.

A canal boat called Shy Swan is coming towards me round a bend. A man at the back is filming a swan that is following it. This swan is certainly not shy – it spots me and decides to follow me instead. I have seen signs on the towpath warning that swans can be aggressive during the nesting season – this one must have a nest in the vicinity. As I walk along, I can hear it motoring through the water behind me, and whenever I stop, it stops. It's obviously got its beady eye on me, and I don't dare look it in the eye. I stop to take a photograph of a man with a chainsaw cutting up a tree blown down in last week's gales, and can sense the swan's presence behind me. After a while it gets out of the water onto the towpath, and I feel even more threatened, but it soon decides that I am not going to harm its nest, and I leave it behind with great relief.

Part of the canal runs alongside a road. Four horse riders pass me.

"How far are you walking?"

"Land's End to John O'Groats."

"Are you?....Really?"

I'm back on the Pennine Way again at Gargrave, up a lane and across some wide open fields. As I reach a stile, a jogger carrying a carrier-bag catches up with me.

"You're going all the way then?"

"Yes."

"I did it myself last year, not this way though" – as he jogs away into the distance.

The Way now follows the River Aire to Airton, where I leave it to go along the road to the inn at Kirkby Malham. I wanted to stay at the Youth Hostel at Malham, but it was fully booked, and this is the only alternative I could find. It is rather expensive, but comfortable. I have an excellent meal to celebrate the fact that I have reached the halfway point of my Journey. I have been walking for four weeks.

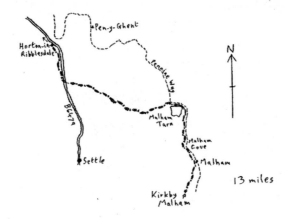

I walk up the road to rejoin the Pennine Way at Malham. This area is obviously very popular – the weekend walkers are out in force. There is a fine Tourist Information building, so I go in and buy some postcards. I sit on a bench outside, write 'HALF WAY!' on each one, and post them to friends and family.

As I follow the road out of the village, a ball rolls across the tarmac in front of me. It belongs to a toddler standing disconsolately behind his garden gate, so I retrieve it for him.

A well-marked footpath leads across the fields towards Malham Cove – not that you could miss it as it is quite an awesome feature. This eighty-metre-high curved limestone cliff was formed by glacial meltwater thousands of years ago. I deviate slightly from the main path to go right up to the base of the cliff – I feel a compulsion to touch it. There is no longer any water coming over the top, instead a stream seeps through underneath the cliff.

The path climbs up a man-made stone staircase at the side of the cliff, emerging at the top on the limestone pavement, deeply marked by channels formed by acid rain. There are

93

hordes of teenagers up here – I suppose that's why the Youth Hostel was full last night.

Paths across the moor lead towards Malham Tarn. It isn't clear which is the Pennine Way, but I am going in the right general direction, so it doesn't matter. It's very bleak up here though – I wouldn't like to be here in fog. Round the tarn it is not so bleak as there are wooded areas along parts of the shoreline. The tarn is one of only eight upland alkaline lakes in Europe. On the north side is Malham Tarn Field Centre, which opened in 1947 to provide professional and leisure courses for people to study the environment. It is quite busy in this area; still lots of walkers about, and cars coming to the Field Centre.

In the tiny village of Water Houses the Pennine Way continues northwards, but I turn west down a country lane. This takes me up and down hills for several miles, then I join a rough track which links up briefly with the Ribble Way to Helwith Bridge. A section of the track has gates across it at both ends, and I am greeted by some friendly horses. I take good care (as always) to secure the gates behind me. At the end of the track a group of motorcyclists seem to be having some trouble with one of their off-road bikes. I'm afraid I don't have a lot of sympathy as these bikes churn up the paths, spoiling the countryside for everyone else. Perhaps I should be more tolerant; walking boots do damage as well, though not as quickly.

As I turn onto the road I notice some coltsfoot flowers in the verge, and ponder that spring seems to be later in these northern climes (or perhaps it's the altitude) – hardly any green is showing on the trees. Further south, a few days ago, spring was bursting out all over, especially the hawthorn hedges. The road leads to the pretty village of Horton-in-Ribblesdale, where the inn does cheap bed-and-breakfast in fairly basic accommodation.

As is so often the case, my mobile phone has no signal, and I have to use the payphone, though I have to wait until someone in the inn has finished using the Internet. I go in the bar to order a meal. The barmaid says I can't order before seven o'clock – I point out that it is ten-past-seven now! Maybe she forgot to put her watch forward last night.

Monday 29/3/2004

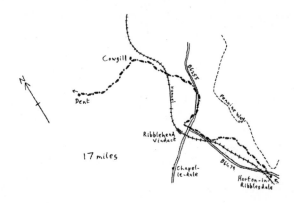

The inn doesn't serve breakfast till half-past-eight, but that's not a problem. I no longer have to worry about reaching my destination after dark, now that the days are getting longer, especially as we are now in British Summer Time. When I'm ready to leave I start going down the stairs, then realise I have left my stick in the bedroom – I can't manage without that!

I stock up on food in the village and get on my way. Where the road turns sharp left, the Pennine Way and Ribble Way join forces and go up the hill to the right. A pleasant country road is straight ahead, and I decide that this is my best option. A short way up the road is the hamlet of New Houses. I don't know how long ago the houses were new, but they look as though they were all built at the same time, and are now maturing nicely. A Pickford's removal lorry is trying to manoeuvre to reverse into a drive, and a lady comes out of a house opposite. She is concerned that it will spoil her grass if it runs over it.

The road peters out at High Birkwith and I follow a path and track back down to the road from Horton-in-Ribblesdale. I am looking forward to seeing the Ribblehead viaduct on the Settle-Carlisle line – this was the reason I took this route.

As I round a bend in the road, I catch my first glimpse of the viaduct, still about a mile away, and manage to get a photo of a train crossing it. At the T-junction there is a parking area for cars, and an information board. This is one of the best places to view the expanse of the viaduct – it is very impressive. Its twenty-four arches span a distance of a quarter of a mile, at a height of 104 feet. It was built in the 1870s by navvies who lived in shanty towns nearby with their families. Over a thousand people died during construction, but many of these were from smallpox. You can get closer to the viaduct by wandering over the moor so I go a little way but it is a deviation from my route.

Up the road to Gearstones I pass a mile-post that declares that it is 34 miles to Richmond. Where's Richmond? – I'll have to check as my geography is not very good. I thought Richmond Hill was in London – now the song is running through my head – 'Sweet lass of Richmond Hill, Sweet lass of Richmond Hill...'

Leaving the road at Gearstones, I join the Dales Way as it climbs to the moor. From here there is an excellent view of Pen-y-Ghent (it sounds like a Welsh name), a 2273-foot fell whose profile resembles a crouching lion. This peak is included in the Pennine Way but I decided not to attempt it – my goal of John O'Groats is more important than hurdles along the way.

The Dales Way crosses the moor then descends a narrow road under a railway viaduct, not as big as Ribblehead viaduct, but quite majestic in its own way. Near here the railway emerges from a one-and-a-half mile tunnel under Blea Moor. It's sad to think that so many railway lines have closed, when they took such a magnificent effort to build in the first place. At least this one was saved from closure – in the 1960s and again in the 1980s.

The road continues into Dentdale, a very pretty valley, where it follows the course of the river Dee, one of at least four in Britain. Eventually I arrive in the village of Dent, where the road becomes a cobbled street. This is deceptive, as it makes you think that it is a pedestrian area, but of course it can't be as it's the only road through the village.

In the centre of the village is a large granite boulder incorporating a drinking fountain. This is a monument to Adam Sedgewick, one of the fathers of modern geology, who was born in the village. Dent is also home to 'The Terrible Knitters of

Dent' – what this actually means is that they were terribly good and terribly fast. Apparently everyone in the village spent most of their time knitting – mostly socks.

My guest house is in the centre of the village, close to the pub where I go for a meal. The landlady lets me use her phone to phone home.

Tuesday 30/3/2004

In the morning we have a pleasant chat. She asks me to send her a postcard when I get to John O'Groats, and knocks £5 off the bill. The lady in the Post Office signs my form, but refuses to stamp it. She says they are not allowed to stamp anything that isn't official – nobody else has had a problem with it.

I go down the road past the church towards the river, and follow the Dales Way along the riverbank. Sheep are grazing in the fields, separated by beautiful wooden gates which look as though they were installed fairly recently. Each gate has a metal tile attached to the gatepost – they appear to have been created from children's clay sculptures, on a nature theme. It is very warm today. I would like to take off my fleece jacket, but it would be extra to carry, so I just unzip it. Spring has definitely arrived in this sheltered valley; even the larches are starting to look green.

Soon the road comes alongside the river. There are no fields in between, so the Dales Way follows the road. Later the Way crosses the river and heads northwards, but I stay this side and continue westwards, the road soon petering out into a farm track. Then it's a path over the hill, an old bridge over a disused railway line, and some more roads. At Killington New Bridge there is a nature reserve that looks very pretty, with woodland walks beside the river. A military aircraft is flying low, banking in a turn. It would make a superb photograph, with the mountains as a backdrop, but of course I am not quick enough.

I take a path across the moor, where I am chased by a flock of sheep. Okay, so they are only following me, not chasing me, but they are very persistent. Eventually I persuade them to stop by waving my stick and shouting at them. There are many tracks criss-crossing over the moor, so I use my GPS to check that I am on the right one and continue confidently. When I stop for lunch, I find I have a voice-mail from James at work, so I phone him back to report my progress. Later, when I check the GPS again, I find that I am much further south than I should be. This excellent track has led me astray; I must have missed a fork a long way back. Fortunately I manage to find my way by a different route to the road that I was heading for in the first place.

It was James who provided the final spur to give me the impetus to do the Walk. I had been making plans for some time, working out my route and deciding what I would need to take, so that I would be ready in case I ever found the time to do it. I had mentioned it a few times – he knew it was an ambition of mine. Then one day I made a joking reference to it, and he asked, "Oh yes, when are you going to do that?" Not with the sense of 'When are you going to get off your backside and put your body where your mouth is?', but rather in the nature of a casual enquiry, as if it had already been decided that I was actually going to DO it. So I thought 'Right, I WILL do it', and started making enquiries about taking extra time off work. In the end I had to take a month unpaid leave and the rest out of my annual holiday.

*

Country roads take me round Killington Lake, and over a bridge over the M6, just south of Killington Lake Services. I watch the traffic hurtling by for a while. We drive up and down this road frequently, so next time we pass this spot I'll be able to say 'I walked over that bridge!'.

I send my daughter a text message, and she phones me back for a chat as I pass through the village of Millholme. I have to make sure I check the map while we're talking as I don't want to take the wrong road. The main road through Oxenholme leads to Kendal. Here I am being given accommodation by Terry, another rambler. When I reach a roundabout by the Leisure Centre, I phone her and we arrange to meet by the Town Hall. Terry lives in one of the many 'yards' that are a feature of Kendal – a door leads from the street onto an alleyway, which in turn leads to a secluded area containing several houses and flats. It is nice and peaceful, away from the traffic and the hustle and bustle of the streets. On the way to her house, we go into a shop. Terry has been given some money by a friend, with instructions to buy me some Kendal Mint Cake – yum, yum!

Remember four weeks ago, on the second day of the walk, I had some trouble with my little toe? I have been protecting it every day ever since, just taking the protection off at night. When I take the moleskin off tonight, the toenail comes with it. It is not at all painful, not even sore, and a new toenail is growing underneath.

I have been studying my maps of Scotland, where I'll be in a few days time, and have decided that one of my planned days will be too strenuous. I was going to take the Southern Upland Way from Beattock to Wanlockhead, but it's all up and down (mostly up) and twenty miles – I can manage hills, and I can manage twenty miles, but not both at the same time. Terry brings out a road atlas (my maps only cover a narrow strip) and I decide that Crawford or Abington would be a good alternative. She lets me use the Internet to look for a B&B, and I manage to book one in Crawford.

It will be Easter soon, and I expect to be on the West Highland Way by then. I imagine it will be quite busy so I'd better do some serious booking. The Youth Hostel at

Rowardennan on Loch Lomond is fully booked, so I have to find an alternative. By the end of the evening I have booked more than two weeks ahead, including most of Easter week. It means I won't have any leeway so I'll have to stick to the plan, but at least it's put my mind at rest knowing I won't have to sleep rough.

All this work has left me with very little time to get to know Terry better but she's walking part of the way with me tomorrow so that will be nice.

CHAPTER NINE

I love to go a-wandering
Along the mountain track

A Wainwright was a gentleman whose greatest pleasure was to go a-wandering. He lived much of his life in Kendal, and spent his spare time exploring the Lake District. He wanted to share his love with other people – his Pictorial Guides to the Lakeland Fells, handwritten and illustrated with his own maps and drawings, became classics.

Wednesday 31/3/2004

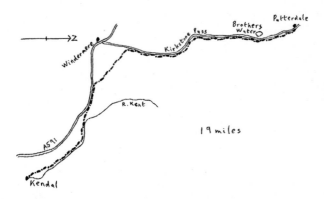

It's my daughter's birthday today, so I send her a 'happy birthday' text message. She responds with 'happy hiking'. Terry cooks scrambled eggs for breakfast and makes me a packed lunch. We discuss this morning's route, and she suggests something different from what I had planned. It doesn't look any further, and is probably flatter and more pleasant, so I bow to her superior knowledge.

She guides me through the town and we take a pleasant

country road to Burneside, then join the Dales Way along the riverbank. It is very pretty here, with lots of violets and wild daffodils. At Staveley we say goodbye and I go on my way alone again. A good footpath beside the main road takes me to Ings, where I follow a lane to the village of Troutbeck, about three miles north of Windermere. There are some lovely blue periwinkles in the hedgerows.

From Troutbeck the main road goes through the Kirkstone Pass to Patterdale, tonight's destination. I was going to go over the mountains – High Street would have been a good route. There's no point in tiring myself out needlessly though as I still have a long way to go and the road through the Pass is steep enough. A stretch of the road has a path running parallel to it through some woodland with lots of holly bushes in it and this makes a pleasant diversion.

Further up I see a sheep on the road, and watch in amazement as it scrambles up and over the top of a six-foot dry-stone wall – I've never seen anything like it. The hillsides are full of sheep – you can't get away from the constant bleating. What is it about sheep? The way they look at you as if they're superior beings, when really they are the most stupid of animals.

At the top of the Pass is the Kirkstone Pass Inn – a very welcome watering-hole! Opposite the inn is the slope of Red Screes, so called because of the colour and looseness of the small stones which cover it. It looks very steep – I find it hard to believe that I actually climbed that in my youth; I certainly wouldn't care to attempt it now.

The road now descends towards Patterdale. Near Brothers Water I see some cows in a field – it makes a pleasant change after all those supercilious sheep. As I approach my farmhouse B&B, I hear two cyclists coming up behind me. They have spotted my sign and one of them shouts "Sponsored walk – WELL DONE!"

I arrive at the farmhouse B&B shortly after six o'clock, just as the sun is disappearing behind the mountains – actual sunset is not until half-past-seven. There is no television in my room, but I find a pile of Reader's Digests in the wardrobe, so after I have written my diary I spend a pleasant evening reading them.

Thursday 1/4/2004

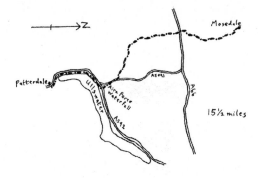

At breakfast time I share a table with a man who is staying here for a few days, for a short walking holiday. He says he walked Land's End to John O'Groats about ten years ago – he gives me a donation, and the landlady knocks a few pounds off the bill.

After calling at the Post Office-cum-shop in the village of Patterdale, I follow the shore of Ullswater, mostly along a footpath between the road and the lake. The daffodils remind me of Wordsworth's poem.

I wandered, lonely as a cloud
That floats on high o'er vales and hills,
When all at once I saw a crowd,
A host, of golden daffodils;

At Glencoyne Park there is a car park and well-maintained footpaths to enable tourists to climb up to the lovely waterfall of Aira Force. It is well worth a visit, and surprisingly busy for a Thursday this early in the year. From the top of the waterfall I continue uphill, up the road to Dockray and High Row. From here an old coach road heads north and then west along the edge of the fell. This is part of the National Cycle Network.

To the north is a stretch of rough, boggy moor called Threlkeld Common. According to the map there is a footpath going straight across it, but I can't find it. I use my GPS to pinpoint my position and set off across the moor from the point that the map indicates. Visibility is very poor as the weather is rather murky. I can just see the mountains behind me and to the left, looming out of the mist, but there are no landmarks at all ahead of me, just featureless moorland. I know there is more than a mile of this, so I check the GPS every hundred paces to make sure I stay on track. Of course the inevitable happens, the batteries run out. The spares are somewhere at the bottom of my rucksack, so I have to stop and rummage for them.

Do you know where you're going to?

Eventually I reach a fence with a stile over it, and signs for the footpath, which looks a lot clearer on the other side. Hooray! What would I do without modern technology! My mind is at rest now, so I sit on the stile to eat my lunch. The path is a lot easier to follow now, and I soon see a wood and a farm which are marked on the map. When I reach the farm track, there is a notice warning that the moor I've just crossed 'may be impassable for horses when wet'.

I follow the farm track and some minor roads, crossing the main A66 between Penrith and Keswick, then up a steep footpath beside a farm.

Do you like the things that life is showing you?

I'm starting to have some strange thoughts about the nature of reality. I still can't quite believe this Adventure is actually happening. Am I really doing this, or is it a figment of my imagination? I spent so long studying the maps when I was doing the planning, that perhaps I'm just dreaming it all. And am I really walking, moving through the country at an amazing rate, or is the ground moving under my feet?

The immediate reality is that I still have about four miles to go, along a pleasant country lane, through Mungrisdale to Mosedale. There is a comfortable hotel here that has a cosy lounge with a bookcase full of interesting books, but no-one is interested in what I am trying to achieve.

Friday 2/4/2004

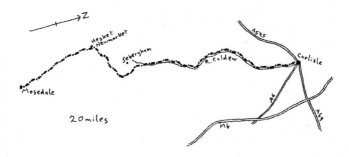

Breakfast *is* at eight-thirty. No leeway! I would have liked it earlier as I have about twenty miles to do today. Never mind, I shouldn't have any problem getting to Carlisle before sunset.

The road is unfenced for the first few miles, with Carrock Fell to my left and open countryside to my right, then it's normal roads to Hesket Newmarket, where I leave the Lake District National Park. Near Sebergham I join the Cumbria Way, which will lead me all the way into Carlisle. A farm track takes me to the bank of the river Caldew, which the Way follows for much of the route.

A man is walking his dog on the other side of the river – the dog is barking. The man sees me and shouts "I wondered what he'd spotted." Just before lunchtime I think 'It's Friday, Mike hasn't phoned yet'. Then just as I sit down on a stile to eat, he phones – he's been busy all morning.

Across a field is a castle called Rose Castle built from a very pretty shade of pink stone. Between here and Bridge End the route leaves the river and goes past a very posh-looking school. Near Bridge End preparations are in hand for a point-to-point meeting.

Beyond Dalston the route is a cycle track alongside the railway line. Willows are being grown commercially here, and there are signs beside the track saying 'BEWARE SPRINKLERS'. The river meanders a bit and the walk is pleasant despite the proximity of the railway. About two miles south of the city centre I pass a factory. I think it's a mill producing animal feed. Beside the path here is a beautiful patch of white violets. There are lots of wild plants growing now, though many are hard to identify before they are flowering. I recognise goosegrass and ground elder, both of which I have tried, without success, to eliminate from my garden.

The Cumbria Way goes right through Carlisle so I don't have to resort to city streets until I'm looking for my B&B. I ask a newspaper vendor for directions, but he's not very sure. He keeps repeating "Victoria Place... Victoria Place..." He does manage to point me in the right general direction though, and I get there eventually. After settling in I go back into the town centre for some chips.

CHAPTER TEN

You tak' the high road
And I'll tak' the low road
And I'll be in Scotland afore ye

Saturday 3/4/2004

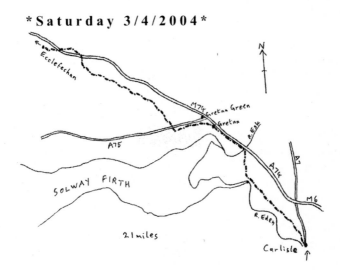

Brian will be staying with me in Ecclefechan tonight. He'll be taking the high road (M6, A74, M74), so I think he'll be there before me. The advantage of taking the minor roads and doing it on foot is that you see a lot more.

*

On my way into Carlisle town centre to get my form stamped, I pass a row of old terraced houses with tiny front gardens, about three feet wide. One has a magnificent magnolia tree in it – that's definitely worth a photograph. A roundabout on the road out of town has pedestrian underpasses and a lovely open area with flowerbeds in the middle. The entrances to the underpasses have been painted with fine murals. Beyond the roundabout are a leisure centre and a large park with sports facilities beside the river Eden. The top of a dry ski slope is just the other side of the hedge next to the road and some children there say hello.

I now follow side roads out of town, past a village called Cargo, to the pretty village of Rockcliffe, beside the river. Brian phones – he's at the last services on the M6, so he'll soon be at Gretna. A long straight road heads towards Metal Bridge, where I briefly join a footpath onto the last section of the Cumbria Coastal Way. This takes me over a high footbridge over the main railway line, and brings me out on the A74 at the Metal Bridge Inn.

Fortunately the road here is not a motorway; there's just a few miles of ordinary dual carriageway between the M6 and the M74. I suppose it would be quite expensive to upgrade it to a motorway, as they would have to leave an ordinary road alongside it, to allow local non-motorway traffic to cross the border without a massive detour. First I cross the river Esk, which joins the river Eden to become the Solway Firth. Now I have two miles of this horrible road before I get to Gretna. There is no footpath or hard shoulder, just a very rough grass verge, and the traffic is thundering by only a few feet away. It is by far the worst bit of road I have walked along in my whole journey up to now.

As I approach Gretna I spot Brian on the bridge over the road, just where the motorway starts. He films me as I walk down the slip road. At the sign that declares 'SCOTLAND welcomes you', we both take photos. It's taken me five weeks to walk through England, and I should get through Scotland in another three weeks.

We go for lunch at the First House cafe. The famous blacksmith's anvil is just up the road at Gretna Green, but weddings are also performed here in the First House. English couples used to elope to Scotland so that they could get married at sixteen without parental consent. Nowadays Gretna is used as a romantic location for a wedding – as I am leaving I see a horse and carriage with a bride on her way to the ceremony.

Brian drives away to find tonight's B&B, and I carry on

alone into Gretna village to do some shopping. It gets very windy and there are a couple of heavy squally showers as I head west and then north along minor roads. I have a few miles to do yet, through Hollee and past Kirtlebridge. A man in a car asks the way to Middlebie, but I can't help him, though when I check the map later I see it's not far away. A heavy hailstorm starts as I cross the bridge over the motorway, and I'm quite wet by the time I arrive in Ecclefechan.

The B&B is opposite the birthplace of Thomas Carlyle, 1795-1881, who was best known as a writer, but was also a mathematician.

Brian has made himself comfortable in the lounge and is watching sport on the television. After I've had my bath we drive to a local hotel for an excellent meal. It feels really strange being in the car – it's the first time I've been in any vehicle since February!

Sunday 4/4/2004 Week 6

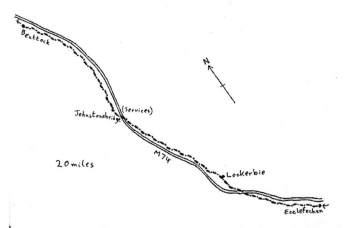

My granddaughter in Aberdeen likes to come and stay with us for holidays. She's coming down for Easter even though I'm not at home. The usual routine is that my son fetches her down to the border and we drive up to pick her up, so we're planning to meet up somewhere today.

I set off up the road, past the statue of Thomas Carlyle. This is the old A74, now a B road, running parallel to the newer M74 – or to be precise, the A74(M). It's quite a pleasant road to walk along, being largely traffic-free with a cycle track at the side. A few miles later I am coming into Lockerbie and two cyclists pass me. One shouts "Good luck!" – "Thank you," I reply. "Keep going," he shouts.

This is the town where the bombed airliner fell out of the sky on 21st December 1988 killing everybody on board and eleven people on the ground, completely obliterating one house and seriously damaging several others. I remember it well, because we drove past the scene the following day, on our way from our (then) home near Aberdeen to stay with family in North Wales for Christmas. A contraflow system was in operation on the dual carriageway, and the place looked like a war zone. A huge mound of earth blocked the southbound carriageway, thrown up from the crater formed by a section of the plane. Behind the mound was a burnt-out car, which I don't believe was ever mentioned by the news reports. The thing I found really annoying about the TV News on the day it happened, was the way they went on and on for about twenty minutes, even though all they actually *knew* could be told in two minutes.

Newsreader: "So what do you think happened here?"

Expert: "Well, we don't really know yet......." and so on.......

*

Brian meets me in Lockerbie and we search for a toilet. Shortly afterwards my son phones to say that he has passed Abington, so we arrange to meet at Johnstonebridge. Brian takes a photo of me at the point I've reached then drives me to the services where we have lunch with my son and granddaughter. Then we go back to Lockerbie so that I can be dropped off at the same point – I'm determined not to cheat!

I say goodbye to Brian and my granddaughter and carry on

walking, up the same road that I've been up and down in the car – rather tedious, but necessary. I still have fourteen miles to go today, and it's after one o'clock, so I have to get a move on. I could take a more interesting route, but I haven't really got time. A Penton's lorry passes me, still on the B road. They are based in Oswestry and Brian used to work for them. I arrive in Beattock before dark, and am pleased to see the little white church – we used to see it every time we drove up this road, but you can't see it from the motorway.

The B&B provides me with an excellent meal of salmon and strawberries. The bathroom is fitted out for disabled people, with a wheel-in shower. In the bedroom is a radio with a cassette player, and I am able to play my tape of Jimmy Logan, which I have carried all the way from Land's End as a good luck charm. It would have been his birthday today.

Monday 5/4/2004

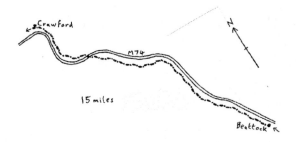

This is the day when I was originally intending to go over the hills to Wanlockhead. My maps don't cover all of my route to Crawford, but I know that the old road follows the motorway in a fairly direct line, and if I arrange the maps I have in order, I can estimate the distance quite accurately. It looks about fifteen miles.

Shortly after setting out, I see a rainbow arching above the road in front of me. This has to be a good omen – it reminds me of other rainbows, previously mentioned in this tale. Rainbows mean sunshine and showers, of course, and that is certainly today's weather, with a cold wind against me – the warm hat comes in useful, I've hardly worn it up to now.

Although this road is rather bleak, it is quite interesting to walk along, seeing all the things we used to drive past before the motorway was built. I find the place known as 'the hole in the wall', where a railway bridge crosses the road. There used to be a long lay-by that went away from the road here, we often used to stop for a picnic lunch to break up a long journey. One end of the lay-by is blocked now, and the whole area looks rather neglected. Strangely, there is a port-a-loo under the bridge, so I take advantage of it.

A man is sitting in the wooded area beside the road, and I wonder what he is doing, but further on I pass a parked car with a sticker in the window – 'Habitat Surveyor' – that must be him. A man in a 'First Engineering' van barely looks up from reading his newspaper, but later, as I approach Crawford, he drives past and offers me a lift.

The old road used to be a dual carriageway, but has been narrowed to a single carriageway. In some places there are narrow cycle lanes both sides of the road, in other places one carriageway has been converted to a wide cycle lane, with an extended central reservation. Often the original white lines can still be seen, including a place where they cross the driveway of a house, complete with a cat's eye. Near Crawford is an out-of-date green road sign which says 'Carlisle A74'.

When I get to Crawford I assume that I must be nearly at my destination, but I find that, although Crawford is only a village, it is a very *long* village! I have to walk another mile, right to the far end of the road, before I reach the B&B. On the way I pass a transport cafe, and think I will have to walk back to it to get a meal, but the landlord tells me there is a good truck stop a hundred yards further along. My daughter phones while I'm eating my meal there. Later I ring some ramblers in the Lanarkshire area, and make arrangements to meet two ladies who want to accompany me between Lanark and Motherwell.

CHAPTER ELEVEN

I sing of a river
I'm happy beside
The song that I sing is the song of the Clyde

Tuesday 6/4/2004

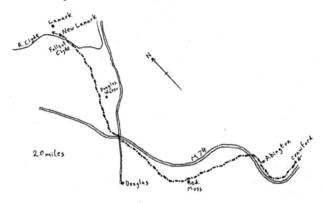

I crossed the young river Clyde yesterday, just before getting to Crawford. Its source is in the hills further south. It would be nice to follow it all the way to Glasgow, but that is not practicable. Never mind, I'll be meeting it again later.

I carry on, still up the old road, and through the pleasant village of Abington where I get phone calls from Brian and my mother. Near the services, the road crosses the motorway and then deviates away from it, following a parallel course about half a mile away, out of sight. This makes it feel more lonely, and this section is very bleak, with open moorland all around. The road is dead straight for three miles, and the Red Moss Truck-stop comes into view. We used to pass it in the old days. It is still in business; the truckers know the best places to go, and leaving the motorway doesn't mean any extra mileage. I go in for a sandwich, although it's not really lunchtime yet.

At Junction 12 near Douglas, the road goes under the motorway, and here I finally part company with my companion of nearly three days, following a minor road towards Lanark. Tom from work phones to see how I'm getting on. The road leaves a wooded area and passes through pleasant countryside overlooking the valley of Douglas Water. A village of the same name is the other side of the valley. Eventually I reach the bank of the river Clyde, much wider than when I left it earlier, swelled by many tributaries.

My map shows a bridge over the river where the road ends, and a footpath beyond, but it's not clear whether it is a public right of way. If it's not, I'll have a two-mile detour to get to New Lanark. I meet a man exercising his dog – I stop to talk to him and he puts my mind at rest about the bridge.

The bridge is at the top of the Falls of Clyde, a magnificent series of waterfalls immortalised in oils by the artist Turner. I can't resist taking lots of photographs. There is a power station at the bottom but it is unobtrusive. The woodland in the area is properly managed, with well-maintained footpaths. The RSPB have an information point here. They have set up a telescope, trained on the cliff face on the other side of the river where a peregrine falcon is nesting. The mother bird is sitting on the nest and the clarity is amazing.

I drop down into New Lanark and easily find the Scottish Youth Hostel in one of the restored buildings of the village.

The village of New Lanark with its cotton mills was built in the late eighteenth century, the mills continuing to function for nearly two-hundred years. This was an ambitious project, started by David Dale. It was purchased in 1799 for £60,000 by his son-in-law Robert Owen, who was an avid social reformer, building schools and preventing younger children from working in the mills. The whole village has been stunningly restored and is now a World Heritage Site.

There is no mobile phone signal in the hostel. I walk a mile up the hill into Lanark to look for food, deciding on a pizza that I start to eat as I walk along, while it's still hot. There's a signal here so I phone Brian. I can't finish the pizza tonight so I leave it in the cupboard, and relax in this recently modernised hostel. There is a cosy TV lounge with shelves full of books, and the sleeping accommodation is excellent. I have a two-bed room to myself, with its own toilet and shower.

Wednesday 7/4/2004

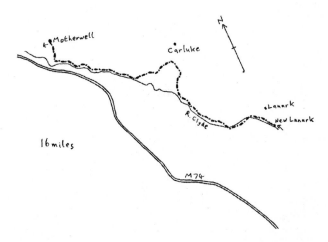

Today I am meeting two ladies who want to help me find my way along the Clyde Walkway, all the way from New Lanark to Motherwell. But first I finish off the rest of the pizza for breakfast, and ask the nice people in reception to book me a bed at the two Scottish Youth Hostels in the Great Glen, one at Laggan and one beside Loch Ness. When I come back downstairs after picking up my gear from the bedroom, Carris and Phyllis are waiting for me in the lobby.

The Clyde Walkway is not properly marked on the map, as it is fairly new. Some footpaths are marked, but it isn't clear how they link up, so I am looking forward to being guided by ladies with local knowledge. We set off along a woodland path close to the river, through Castlebank Park, where the Walkway is marked with the usual wooden posts. At Kirkfieldbank we have to cross the river and proceed along the road for a mile or so, before re-crossing to a riverbank path. We reach a park at Crossford, where a miniature railway is being refurbished. Here the waymarkers suddenly stop. My new friends are confused because they thought that the Walkway was continuous all the way to Glasgow, but they haven't walked it before.

We manage to find an unmarked path not far from the river. This leads us to a group of houses, where we meet a lady getting into a car. Carris knows her so we stop to chat. She tells us that the Clyde Walkway has not been completed in this area, and gives us some useful information about possible routes we could take. We follow roads up the hill, away from the river, and come within a mile of Carluke before turning and finding a path over Jock's Burn, leading to a golf course. Then it's a main road back down towards the river. It's not a pleasant road to walk along – it is straight, the cars are fast, and the narrow grass verge is very uneven.

At Brownlee we find a path through the woods, which leads down to the river where we re-join the Clyde Walkway. It is properly waymarked again now, through the woods and beside the river. We follow it all the way to Motherwell, where we leave the river and take a path up to Dalzell House, a fine old mansion house which has been converted into posh flats. On the way there are a lot of little yellow flowers, which I later discover to be golden saxifrage.

At Motherwell College, Carris and Phyllis bid me farewell, and wish me luck for the rest of my journey. Tonight I am staying at the Hall of Residence in the College. They don't provide meals, so I go into town to get some supplies, and chicken and chips which I take back to eat in the dining hall. Later I phone another rambler whose group, from Milngavie (pronounced Mull-guy), are planning a walk on the West Highland Way in three days time. I hope to meet up with them at Drymen.

CHAPTER TWELVE

I belong to Glasgow
Dear old Glasgow town

Thursday 8/4/2004

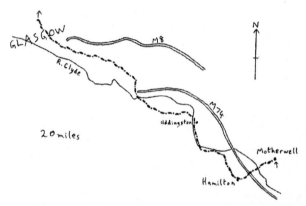

The first part of my route this morning is straight down the main road into Hamilton. There is a good footpath beside the road, which passes Strathclyde Country Park then goes under the M74 at Junction 6. Graceful footbridges take me over the slip roads.

In Hamilton I have to find the local branch of our bank where some forms need signing for some personal business. A traffic warden gives me directions. Business concluded, I continue up another main road to Bothwell Bridge. Here a sign indicates the Clyde Walkway beside the river again, so I follow the path.

There must be a waymarker missing – I soon find myself next to a road away from the river. There was a path that could have been the correct one, but it looked as though it was over private ground. Now I have to find my way round the streets of Blantyre, getting back to the river at the David Livingstone Centre, the birthplace of the famous explorer.

A footbridge crosses the river, and I am back on the Clyde Walkway in tranquil woodland. A mile further on I pass Bothwell Castle, which is largely in ruins, partly as a result of many sieges during the wars with England.

At Uddingston I cross the river on a footbridge/cycle track beside the railway, and stop for something to eat. Before I started the Adventure, I contacted various newspapers and radio stations to try and get some publicity. My photograph and story were printed in local papers, and a local radio station gave me a brief mention. I thought the *Daily Record*, a Glasgow newspaper, might be interested because of the Jimmy Logan connection, but they didn't reply to my e-mail. I phone them now, as I am nearly in Glasgow. They say they will phone me back if they've got room in the paper for my story, but nothing comes of it.

Soon after this, the Walkway disappears again, and I lose some time investigating a path through a wooded area surrounding an old brickworks. Another path has a sign 'dangerous footbridge closed'. I think it would have led over a tributary back to the bank of the river Clyde. I give up and find a different route along minor roads through Newton and Westburn, where I get my usual weekly call from Mike – it's only Thursday but it's Good Friday tomorrow so he'll be on holiday. Then a main road takes me into the fringes of Glasgow.

Along Tollcross Road, opposite the park, is a fine terrace of Victorian Glasgow tenements. Many of the entrances now have security doors with access intercoms, but some are still open and you can see the original tiling in the lobby and the stairs leading up to the individual flats.

Then I come to a shopping area where all the shops have metal shutters. It looks a rough area – I wouldn't like to be here after dark. There are plenty of people about, but I am on my guard, personal alarm at the ready. An oldish man comes alongside me, saying, "That's a fine stick."

"Yes, it's handy," I reply, implying I could use it if I had to. He admires the deer antler, and asks me about my sponsored walk – he has seen the sign on my rucksack. He puts his hand in his pocket and gives me a pound coin. His parting words are

"Don't rush on, keep it steady."

Jimmy Logan was born in Glasgow, in a street called Inglis Street in Dennistoun. I can work it into my route without increasing the mileage, and it will be nice to see where he was born. As I turn the corner into the street, I am dismayed to see that the houses have all been demolished – the whole street is just a piece of waste ground.

I continue into the city centre and get my form stamped at the Post Office. It feels strange walking along Sauchiehall Street among all the shoppers, in my boots and rucksack, my stick tap-tapping along the pavements. When I get to the hostel, I am embarrassed to find that I can't get my purse out of my pocket to pay the landlord – the tag on the zip has broken. I change into my spare trousers and manage to open the zip, then make a new tag using the cord off my compass.

The TV in the lounge doesn't work very well, so I read magazines instead, and chat to a young couple who are staying here. They tell me about a man who climbed Ben Nevis every day for forty years, to check the weather station.

Friday 9/4/2004

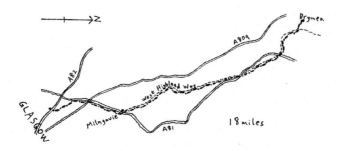

The Botanic Gardens are only half a mile from the hostel, and once again, I can include it in my route without adding any mileage. I feel strangely lonely as I stand looking at the young flowering cherry tree in the middle of a rose garden. A plaque explains that it was planted in memory of Jimmy Logan. It isn't in flower yet – even the leaf buds are not quite bursting. In a way, today is the anniversary of his death three years ago, as it was Good Friday, but the date is different. I suppose one reason for my feeling of loneliness is that I had hoped to get the media involved at this point, but they weren't interested. Still, it's nice to stand and meditate quietly.

The Kelvin Walkway starts at the back of the Botanic Gardens. This follows the river Kelvin to Milngavie. It meanders quite a bit, so I won't be following it all the way. It's a useful starting point though, and I follow it for about a mile, to the place where the Forth and Clyde canal crosses the river via an aqueduct. Here I have to decide between river and canal, and finally plump for canal. This is quite interesting, though not as picturesque as the river – it is built alongside a dismantled railway line and passes a gas works and other industrial paraphernalia.

I leave the canal after a mile, and head up the main road to Milngavie. The office of Ochre, one of my chosen charities for the Walk, is not far from here, in Bearsden. It would be nice to pop in and see them and it would only be a small diversion. However, when I phone, I am not surprised to find that there's nobody there today, as it's Good Friday.

Milngavie has a very nice pedestrianised town centre. As I arrive, a Walk of Witness is setting off from the clock, led by a man carrying a large wooden cross. I linger for a while, looking for somewhere to eat. It's a bit early for lunch, but I manage to buy a hot-dog and cake. The Walk of Witness comes back to its starting point after a while, and I am given donations by an old lady following it, and a man doing some shopping.

The West Highland Way starts here, marked by a fine granite obelisk with the logo of the West Highland Way, a stylised thistle within a hexagon. After leaving the town, the Way passes through Mugdock Wood, where several concrete slabs with carved inscriptions are set into the path – 'Drumclog moor new leaves unfurling', 'Mugdock Wood many years turning', 'breathe'.

The path passes a pond that, in a few weeks time, will be ablaze with yellow irises, if my identification of the leaves is correct. The countryside becomes more open as I pass Craigallian Loch. Just past here are some wooden houses that I assume are holiday homes, but someone tells me later that they were built in the Second World War without planning permission, and are lived in permanently. The council can't force demolition so long as they are maintained to a proper standard.

After a short stretch along the road, the Way turns up a hill, where all I can see ahead is a high stone wall. I wonder what is beyond, and how I'm going to get there! As I approach, I see stone slabs sticking out of the wall – oh, no, it's one of those horrible stone stiles! I negotiate this with some difficulty, but find that the effort was well worth it, as I am greeted by the most fantastic vista. It is definitely one of those 'Wow!' moments. In the foreground is open countryside with a few scattered cottages and a small hill. In the distance, all along the horizon, are the mountains of the Trossachs, some fifteen to twenty miles away. The weather is fine and the view is crystal clear. I take photographs, but I doubt whether my basic camera will do justice to this magnificent sight.

Three walkers pass me. Later on I re-pass them several times – I'm playing hare and tortoise again. Spring has overtaken me here; the bursting buds of the larches look like tiny green shaving brushes. A section of the path is along an old railway line, the Blane Valley Railway, which linked Lennoxtown and Dumgoyne, forming part of the route from Glasgow to Aberfoyle. Alongside is a pipeline, carrying water from Loch Lomond to Central Scotland.

I meet two ladies and a gentleman who are taking a short walk on this easy section, and we get talking. The man says he saw me this morning on the road in Anniesland, just after I left the canal – he recognises my yellow fleece. We talk about Jimmy Logan, and he says he worked with him at Loch Fyne after he'd got cancer.

Eventually I arrive at Drymen. The landlady is out, so her

husband feeds me milk and biscuits, and we sit chatting at the kitchen table. Later I go for a meal at a hotel in the village. When I get back, I talk with the landlady for ages, which is most convivial. She is really interested in my Walk, but I have to make my excuses as I have my diary to write.

CHAPTER THIRTEEN

On the bonnie, bonnie banks o' Loch Lomond

Saturday 10/4/2004

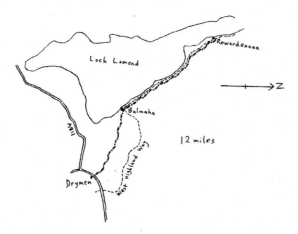

The landlady gives me a donation before I leave to meet the Milngavie Ramblers at a cafe in the village. There are about eighteen of them. We talk over coffee and they collect nineteen pounds for me. One of them takes a group photograph – he promises to send me a copy and says it will be in their local paper.

Their walk today will take them along a section of the West Highland Way, over Conic Hill and finishing at Balmaha on the shore of Loch Lomond. I would love to accompany them, but I feel it is more prudent to conserve my energy by going along the road to Balmaha, as I have another seven miles or so to do after that. They agree that it would be foolish to do more than I need to, and they wish me luck as we go our separate ways. A few minutes later some of them wave as they pass me in cars – they have to take some cars to Balmaha so that they have got transport when they finish their walk. It's one of the problems of doing a linear, rather than circular, walk in a rural area with not much public transport – we used to call it 'doing a shuttle' in my days with the Stonehaven Ramblers.

I have quite a short day today, about twelve miles, so I linger a bit when I get to Balmaha, and look at the pleasure boats moored at the side of the Loch. The West Highland Way climbs over an outcrop of rock, and I decide I can manage this bit – it's worth it for the views of Loch Lomond. The rest of the way to Rowardennan I mostly stick to the road, just following the Way where it doesn't add much distance.

A girl carrying a large pack overtakes me. Her boots are hanging on her pack and she is wearing trainers – she explains that this is because she is suffering from blisters. Later I pass a lad carrying the most enormous pack I've ever seen, with cooking utensils and other camping equipment dangling from it. He appears to be struggling, and tells me that this is the first expedition he has attempted since suffering a leg injury. I hope he isn't overdoing it.

I arrive in the village of Rowardennan mid afternoon. There isn't much here apart from a hotel, a Youth Hostel, and a few houses, but the place is heaving with cars and people. This is the furthest extent of the road on the eastern side of the Loch – there's just a track beyond. Once again there is no signal on my phone. The landlord at my B&B lets me try his mobile, as his landline isn't working at the moment – he is on a different network and it works by the back door.

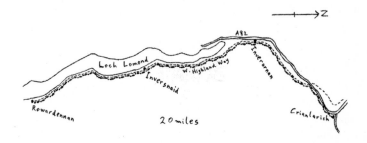

Today I shall be following the eastern shore of Loch Lomond even more closely than yesterday, right up to its northernmost tip. It starts off as an easy track through sheltered woodland. The steep bank to my right is punctuated by a number of gills, just small trickles, with a wealth of different mosses and lichens. On the left are rocks, covered in moss, some with shallow-rooted trees growing on top. The sycamore trees are just coming into leaf, and wood-sorrel is sprouting everywhere, some already flowering, looking like pearls among the bright green leaves.

At Inversnaid is a hotel, normally reached by a road that comes from an easterly direction and finishes here. Tourists can take boat trips from the jetty and a passenger ferry crosses the loch. I get a text from Pauline, the art teacher, asking how I'm getting on. 'On the shore of Loch Lomond – fantastic', I reply. 'Great, R U going to write a book about it?' – 'Hoping to'. Ah, the wonders of modern technology! While I've got a signal, I phone my son to make arrangements for next weekend, when my granddaughter is going back home to Aberdeen.

It being Easter Sunday, there are lots of tourists about. Many of them are trying part of the footpath, which is still the West Highland Way. It is quite difficult in this area, with rocks to scramble over. Some groups of people are talkative, and I am given several donations.

125

I find that the rocks slow me down considerably, so I decide not to visit Rob Roy's Cave. Rob Roy MacGregor was born in 1671. He became an outlaw when one of his cattle deals went wrong, the drover having run off with money borrowed from the Duke of Montrose. Visiting his cave would take too long and a lot of extra scrambling, and someone tells me there's not much to see anyway. I don't want to take any more risks than necessary – it would be a shame to sprain an ankle or something at this stage, especially on an unplanned diversion.

At one point the only way forward is along a rock ledge, about eighteen inches wide and five yards or so long. On the right is a wall of rock and on the left a steep drop to the loch. One slip and you're in big trouble. It's scary but I just have to grit my teeth and go for it.

The tourists have gradually petered out – only the serious walkers are left. The only other company is a herd of feral goats with young kids. These are descended from escapees during the Highland Clearances in the eighteenth and nineteenth centuries. The path gets easier as I get nearer to the top of the loch, and there is a refreshing shower of light rain – it's been quite warm today.

I have a meal at a farm with a campground near Inverarnan. It's teatime already, but I still have miles to go. At least the days are longer now so I should get there before dark. The path follows Glen Falloch. It goes up and down quite a lot, but is pleasant walking. The Falls of Falloch are pretty, although you can't get close to them. Near a farm, a herd of Limousin calves is wandering about on the path, which is alongside the river now.

The West Highland Way crosses the main road and goes up the hill. It is getting late so I decide to stay on the road for the last couple of miles. A motorist stops and asks if this is the road to Tarbet. I tell her I think it's in the opposite direction. I discover later that there are several places of that name, but the one that she wanted was probably the one on the western shore of Loch Lomond, and she had almost certainly just driven through it!

I eventually arrive at the Scottish Youth Hostel in Crianlarich at eight o'clock, and find that I have to sleep in a top bunk – that's no problem as there's a chair to climb up by.

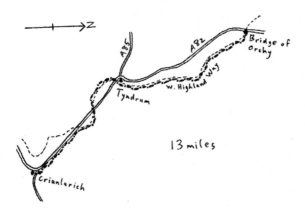

At breakfast time I go to reception to see what the small shop can offer in the way of provisions, as the hostel is self-catering. The choice is very limited, but I don't want to waste time by walking to the village shop and back, so I decide on a tin of rice pudding. This may sound a strange choice for breakfast, but I enjoy it, and it is filling and nutritious.

When I get on my way, I call at the village shop to stock up. A foreign couple is in there. They ask if they can change Euros, but the shopkeeper is unable to oblige. The banks are closed today as it is Easter Monday, so they are advised to go to the Green Welly Stop at Tyndrum, a few miles up the road.

I continue up the road myself, that being easier than climbing the hill to join the West Highland Way – it will come down to meet me later anyway. A house in the village has an old church bell sitting in the garden. I'm envious; I collect ornamental bells and something like that would make a fine addition to my collection.

After a couple of miles, the West Highland Way crosses the main road and I join it on a track past St Fillan's Priory. St Fillan was an Irish evangelist who came to Scotland in the seventh century, travelled extensively, and lived to an old age, eventually being buried in Strathfillan. The monastery that was founded here in the twelfth century was made into a priory by Robert the Bruce in 1318. A Holy Pool in the river Fillan nearby is said to cure insanity. Fillan's staff and bell are now kept in the National Museum of Antiquities in Edinburgh.

At Dalrigh (which means King's Field), a wooded area beside the river is undergoing extensive maintenance – trees being planted, new paths being made. It looks a bit untidy at the moment, but should be lovely when it's settled down. Nearby is a secluded lochan, or small loch. A notice declares that the sword of Robert the Bruce is reputed to lie beneath its dark waters.

Tyndrum is a large village at the junction of three main roads on the tourist trail. It has hotels, shops, pubs, and the Green Welly Stop, a complex of gift shops, restaurant, take-away and filling station. It is heaving with tourists on this Holiday Monday. I go in the restaurant for a meal, but it is very busy – I wish I'd gone for a pub meal instead.

I am surrounded by mountains now, many of them Munros, that is Scottish mountains over three-thousand feet. I have no intention of climbing any of them. The path runs parallel to the road and the railway, making use of an old military road for much of the way to Bridge of Orchy. Three paragliders are floating high above – how did they get up there? Did they have to climb the mountain first, or were they dropped by an aeroplane? The railway makes a wide loop, following the contours as far as possible, crossing small valleys on viaducts.

After a few more miles of similar scenery, I arrive at the small village of Bridge of Orchy. The hotel here has a bunkhouse attached to it. This is like a hostel with dormitories and shower rooms, except there are no cooking facilities or sitting rooms. I actually have a signal on my phone (this is getting to be a rare occurrence), so I phone my mother to report progress, and send my daughter a text. She phones back for a chat. I tell her how all this walking has become a way of life – the days and the weeks are meaningless, timeless.

CHAPTER FOURTEEN

Raindrops keep
falling on my head
But that doesn't mean my eyes will soon be turning red,
Crying's not for me....

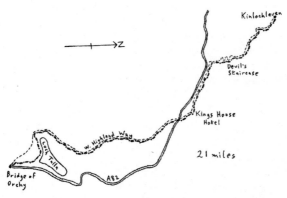

The hotel provides breakfast in the bar for the occupants of the bunkhouse. It's supposed to be at eight o'clock, but they're a bit late opening the doors – all the walkers are gathered outside waiting. A young foreigner complains that he doesn't want to be delayed too much, as he has thirty-two kilometres to do today. I remark that I have twenty-one miles. "Is same thing, I think," he replies. "Kinlochleven?" – "Yes." Everyone is doing the West Highland Way.

After breakfast I don my waterproofs as the weather is rather damp this morning. The Way follows the old military road over the hill, but I decide it will be easier, though slightly longer, to follow the road round the valley, alongside the river Orchy to Loch Tulla. A large sign warns, 'That which burns never

129

returns'. I think it would be quite hard to start a forest fire this weather!

I join up with the Way again at Inveroran, as it proceeds up the Old Glencoe Road. This was built by Telford in the early 1800s to replace the military road. It is a fine paved track that marches across Rannoch Moor with gusto. I have to pace myself today as I have so far to go, but I am making good progress. The moor is very open, which means that there is absolutely nowhere to find a 'convenient' spot, especially with all these people about, playing hare and tortoise again. Also it is getting wetter by the minute. By the time I reach King's House Hotel I am dripping wet, hungry, and desperate for the toilet.

King's House Hotel dates from the seventeenth century, and is one of the oldest licensed inns in Scotland. Its name comes from the time, after the Battle of Culloden in 1745, when it was used as barracks for King George III's troops. Later it was used by drovers, and by workmen on their way to the building of the dam at the Blackwater Reservoir.

Being so isolated, it is now like an oasis in the desert for wet and weary walkers on the West Highland Way. It has a walkers' bar, furnished with simple wooden benches and tables, providing cheap tasty meals. A large bowl of leek and potato soup goes down well. Some of the walkers that I keep passing are in here, including a man (possibly Dutch?) with an orange pennant sticking out of his rucksack on a long pole that catches on the doorframe.

Suitably refreshed, I venture back out into the rain and continue plodding on. We are on the old military road again, which, although paved, is a lot rougher and narrower than the Old Glencoe Road. The hardest part is the Devil's Staircase, which climbs steeply up the hillside by means of a seemingly endless series of zigzags. I am surprised how easily I get to the top – I must be a lot fitter than I was six weeks ago.

The path beyond is rockier, but at least it's mostly downhill now. Across the moor I can just make out the Blackwater Reservoir through the mist. The dam was built to supply water to the hydro-electric plant at the aluminium smelter, one of the largest in the world, at Kinlochleven. The village was purpose-built for the workers. Eventually the path comes out on a modern track that leads down past the aluminium works, which are closed now, the villagers turning to walkers and tourists for a new source of income.

I am in Kinlochleven now, and am not sure where tonight's B&B is. A man walking his dog gives me directions, and I soon arrive at the house, where the landlady spreads newspaper for me to drip on while I take my boots off. My boots are soaked so I stuff newspaper into them. The rain hasn't permeated my waterproofs though, except at the wrist, neck and ankles – at least my underwear is dry! I manage to have a bath here – the first since Ecclefechan ten days ago, everywhere else has just had showers.

In the lounge a couple are watching television. They are on holiday from County Antrim in Ireland, and we make conversation over the light refreshments provided by the landlady.

* W e d n e s d a y   1 4 / 4 / 2 0 0 4 *

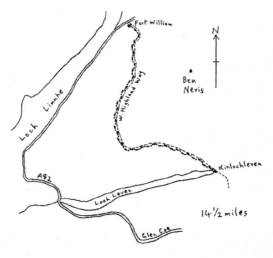

It's still raining this morning; I don't think it's stopped all night. I've got a relatively short day today, so I delay my departure in the hope that the rain will ease off. It doesn't. I then waste twenty minutes looking for a shop to replenish my supplies, which are getting low. I can't find one – why didn't I ask the landlady?

I give up, and follow a steep path up through woodland, still on the West Highland Way. The burns are all swollen with so much continuous rain and are raging torrents. The path leaves the wood and joins a track that continues for long, lonely miles through the glen of Lairigmor. It's the old military road again. But where are all those people I saw yesterday? Have they given up and gone home? Perhaps they're ahead of me as I was late starting. I did see a few in Kinlochleven while I was wasting time, but they're nowhere to be seen now. After a while I catch up with a Belgian couple, and have a chat with the girl.

There's not a lot to see in this desolate glen – a couple of ruined cottages, a few sheep, two dead lambs. The scenery is majestic though, or it would be if the weather was better. You have to use your imagination. It's very wet underfoot – I seem to be walking in rivers much of the time.

By noon the weather is really starting to get to me. Do you ever talk to people inside your head? Sometimes I have imaginary conversations with Jimmy Logan:-

"Aw, Jimmy, can't you do something about this rain?"

"I've got no control over the weather!"

"I suppose not......Maybe you could just have a word......?"

"I'll see what I can do."

Yes I know it's mad, but it makes me feel better. Strangely enough, the rain stops shortly afterwards, then becomes light intermittent showers with a drying wind.

The track turns northwards and enters a forest, where I stop and finish off my meagre supplies. I'm still hungry. Fortunately I'll be in Fort William tonight and there should be plenty of shops there. A notice board beside the track indicates that there is a choice of routes to the town – the track on the left will enter the town from the west while the footpath on the right will come in from the east. The latter is the route of the West Highland Way, so I stick to that.

The bulk of Ben Nevis comes into view on my right – I

certainly don't have time to climb that! I continue downhill through the forest. I am fascinated by the colour of the moss under the conifers – it is bright green and looks almost luminous; somehow it has an alien feel to it. Further down, foxgloves and wild raspberry canes are sprouting in profusion, though of course neither is flowering yet.

Below me, on the road, I can see the Scottish Youth Hostel. I'm glad I decided not to stay there tonight, it's more than two miles from the shops. The Way drops down to the road and eventually finishes at the roundabout, where a sign declares 'THE END OF THE WEST HIGHLAND WAY'. I am about to take a photo of it when a girl sitting on a bench offers to take my photo standing next to it, saying that it's quite an achievement to walk the West Highland Way. I explain that I've actually come a bit further than that!

The fort that gave Fort William its name was built about 1690, the name being in honour of King William of Orange. It was demolished in the nineteenth century to make way for the railway.

The road into town is decorated with flowerbeds in the shape of dolphins leaping over waves – a very pretty addition to a rather uninspiring town. I arrive at the Backpackers' Hostel near the town centre, where I am told I am in the Little Misses' room, and am allocated Miss Splendid's bed. This is unusual as most hostels just tell you the room number, and it's first come, first served for the beds. It's an excellent hostel, with a comfortable lounge and lots of friendly notices everywhere. After settling in, I visit the nearest supermarket and buy plenty of food. I'll be in hostels again for the next two nights, and they're all self-catering. When I get back I soon satisfy my hunger.

I'm never going to stop the rain by complaining,
Because I'm free, nothing's worrying me.

Thursday 15/4/2004

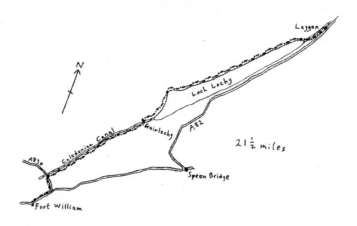

Last night when I got to Fort William, I discovered I had a voice mail from James. It was too late to phone him back, as he would have gone home. I phone this morning, and Sophie, another team member, answers, so I give her an update on my progress.

After a good breakfast, mostly out of a tin, I get on my way. It is raining quite heavily again. Today I am following the Great Glen Way, which is partly the same as the Great Glen Cycle Route. I retrace my steps to the roundabout and follow the main road round to Banavie. We stayed at a B&B here once, many years ago, when the children were young. Here the road goes over a swing bridge, near the start of the Caledonian Canal, designed by Thomas Telford and constructed between 1803 and 1822.

The cycle route joins the towpath of the canal, and I climb up beside Neptune's Staircase, a series of fine locks raising the canal to the necessary level. It's easy walking now for several miles. There are a lot of gorse bushes in this area, many of them in flower – an old saying asserts that 'When gorse is out of bloom, kissing's out of fashion'. This refers to the fact you'll always find a few of the bright yellow flowers at any time of

134

year. Most of the trees beside the canal are covered in a sort of furry lichen of a greyish-green colour.

I turn to look at the mountains that I came through yesterday, and see that Ben Nevis is covered with a fresh blanket of snow.

The river Lochy flows alongside the canal, joining Loch Lochy to Loch Linnhe, the sea loch at Fort William. At Gairlochy the canal rises through more locks into Loch Lochy, which was raised twelve feet from its original level by the canal engineers. The route goes over the swing bridge, the only original bridge on the canal, still operated by hand. Here the cycle route and the Great Glen Way part company for a while, cyclists having to keep to the road, while walkers can take the prettier route through the woods beside the loch. The two routes join up again on the road, then continue along a forest track, which runs for miles close to the loch – there is no road here. It has stopped raining now and it is getting quite sunny. Someone has painted something beside the track in pink paint – it says 'LOG SEAT'. Presumably it's a marker for workers who will erect one.

At the top end of Loch Lochy, at Laggan, more locks take the canal higher, to a short engineered section. Here the cycle route continues along the forest track, while the Great Glen Way crosses the canal by means of the locks and proceeds along the towpath. A small diversion takes me to the Scottish Youth Hostel, a fine old building in a tranquil setting, despite being beside the main road through the Glen. I manage to find a phone signal in parts of the building, then settle down in the lounge to read magazines – there is no television.

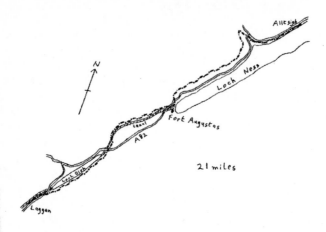

Once again I have a tinned breakfast, then start out alongside the canal to North Laggan, where it enters the next loch in the chain, Loch Oich. The Great Glen Way follows the shore on the south side of the loch. Part of it is on an old railway line, but mostly it takes a parallel path between the overgrown railway and the shoreline. It is a pleasant wooded walk. On the opposite shore can be seen Invergarry Castle, once home of the McDonnel chiefs, now in ruins. It was burned by Government troops after the battle of Culloden in 1746, because McDonnel helped Bonnie Prince Charlie.

At the top end of the loch, another bridge crosses the canal at Aberchalder, and I return to the towpath. Actually I doubt whether 'towpath' is the correct name for it – I don't suppose the Caledonian Canal ever had horse-drawn barges, being built for much larger and grander craft. A short distance further at Cullochy Lock (going downhill now), the path crosses the canal. A man from a boat going through the lock asks me about my walk, and gives me £5.

Now it's several miles along the canal to Fort Augustus, passing another lock on the way. Here the canal descends through a fine flight of locks, and enters Loch Ness under a swing bridge.

Originally called *Cille Chumein*, for the church of St

136

Cummein, Fort Augustus was named after one of the sons of George II, after the Jacobite uprising of 1715. This son became the infamous Duke of Cumberland who subjugated the Highlands after Culloden.

There are lots of tourists about, and I linger for a while, getting a meal from the chip shop and doing some shopping. The lady in the Post Office stamps my form and gives me a donation. Beside the locks is a charming model of the Loch Ness Monster made from wire and plants. I see that the road has been closed, so I watch while the swing bridge opens to let through a beautiful yacht with a tall mast – it will have all the locks to negotiate now.

I follow signs for the Great Glen Way up a back street on the edge of the town. A house has the name 'Edelweiss', and soon the song is running through my head, followed rapidly by all the songs from 'The Sound of Music'. A steep path then takes me on to a forest track again. A little further on, the Great Glen Cycle Route joins me, it had to go on the main road through Fort Augustus.

There are several miles of track now to Invermoriston. Sometimes you can't see much for the trees, but in places there are gaps in the forest, and you have an excellent view of Loch Ness – a view you couldn't get from a car. RAF planes are practising low-level flying below me.

Years ago I bought a self-published book by a man called Alan Profitt, who did the Walk in 1997. He described his route and his method – travelling light and sleeping in a proper bed every night. I decided then that if I ever did it, I would use that method, but would choose my own route. However, our routes have more-or-less coincided since Glasgow, though I think they'll be diverging later. He advises dropping down to the main road about a mile south of Invermoriston, but I ignore this because I don't like main roads. Instead I follow the waymarked route away from the loch, high above the river Moriston with no path down to make it shorter. This adds about two miles to my journey – eventually the path turns back on itself and brings me down into Invermoriston.

After all that extra walking I am too tired to face the steep climb back to the forest track, so I end up on the main road after all, with three miles or so to get to the Youth Hostel. And after spending all that time in the forest, and not seeing any wildlife there, two deer run across the road just in front of me.

The Scottish Youth Hostel at Alltsigh is right beside Loch Ness, in fact my room is in a wooden building virtually on the beach, about ten yards from the water. Great, I can Nessie-watch from the window! (He/she is not about today though – the calm surface of the loch is undisturbed.)

I am sharing my room with an Australian girl who introduces herself as Jackie. She is a doctor and has been working as a locum in Elgin, and is travelling Europe.

CHAPTER FIFTEEN

I love a lassie
A bonnie, bonnie lassie,
She's as pure as the lily in the dell

Saturday 17/4/2004

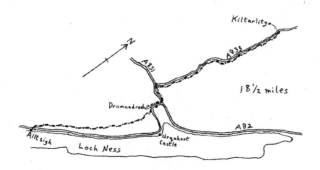

I have a packet of savoury rice for breakfast, and say goodbye to Jackie, who is waiting for a bus to continue her travels. Opposite the hostel is an access point for the forest track. Several tracks and paths are shown on the map, and it's not clear how they join up, so I trust the waymarkers. These take me up a series of zigzags until I am high above Loch Ness, looking back at the hostel in its loch-side setting. Clumps of pale yellow primroses are everywhere on the steep hillside among the trees.

A path that appears to have been made recently leads gradually down to a lower track, which I follow until I reach a fork. My map indicates that the left-hand path leads to a road higher up, which is where I want to get to, so I ignore the way-markers. A short way up I come to a gate with a big sign – 'This is not the Cycle Route, not the Great Glen Way, go back 90 metres and turn left'. However there's no mention of it being private, so I carry on, as I suspect the designated route might take me a long way round. At the end of the path I come out on the road next to a small pottery, and the Great Glen Way actually emerges close by, so I could have followed it after all.

A long straight country road leads down towards Lewiston. I can no longer see Loch Ness, but the mountains beyond are impressive. A farm track has a gate with a printed sign – 'Please shut the gate' – below it a hand painted addition says 'Even if open'.

I follow signs for the Great Glen Way down a pleasant woodland path, but it turns out to be a roundabout way into Lewiston – I'd have been quicker going down the road. When I reach the main road, there are picnic tables beside the river Coiltie, so I rest awhile and have my lunch.

The main road goes through Drumnadrochit. An American lady asks me which is the way to Urquhart Castle, except she can't pronounce Urquhart. It stands on a promontory overlooking Loch Ness, and I have bypassed it, but I'm able to direct her.

Drumnadrochit is quite a touristy place, being home to the Loch Ness Monster Visitor Centre, which we visited a few years ago. I spend a few minutes browsing round the paintings in a souvenir shop. There is also an excellent public convenience.

I leave the village and head west along the road. At Milton I turn north and ascend a steep hill. A lorry passes me – it bears the slogan 'Anyware – Anywhere'. That's rather clever. Now I have a long road across open moorland and a gradual descent towards the village of Kiltarlity.

My granddaughter's Easter holiday has finished – Brian has driven up with her and we're all staying at Kiltarlity tonight. They meet me on the road a couple of miles south of the village. It's great to see them again. They have the address of the B&B but can't find it, and there's no signal on the mobile to phone the landlady. I carry on walking while they try again. When I reach the village they pick me up and eventually we find the house.

After settling in, we go for a meal at a local hotel. Brian has a couple of drinks with his meal, so I drive back to our lodgings.

It feels really weird being behind the wheel again as I haven't driven for seven weeks.

*

In 1999, my granddaughter came to stay with us for the Easter holidays, as usual. She was five then. One day I took her to see my mother in Manchester. On the long drive home she said: -

"Grandma, has your car got a stereo?"

"Yes."

"Why don't you use it?"

"I do sometimes. Do you want some music now?"

"Yes."

So I put the radio on but reception was poor.

"Do you like that?"

"No."

"I'll put a tape on then."

Of course my favourite tape of my idol was in the slot, so I pushed it in. It was halfway through and the first song she heard was *Bonnie Wee Jeannie McCall* – "That's a funny one," she said. When it came to *The Northern Lights of Old Aberdeen*, she said "Grandma, that song's about where I live." At *I Love a Lassie* she got all excited, declaring "That's my song!" I knew what she meant – she'd learnt it in school.

When we got home, Brian met us at the front door – "Granddad, Grandma's music's got my song!", and she sang it for him – "We did it for Valentine's Day." Then, by way of a change, he got her to sit at his drum kit, and she bashed away quite rhythmically.

The next day, she asked me to play 'the music' again. I thought Jimmy Logan would be really pleased to know that a five-year-old was enjoying his songs so much, so I decided it was a good excuse to write to him. I received a lovely reply to my letter – 'Children are wonderful and full of discovery'.

In the summer she stayed with us again. We were walking the dogs on the first day when she started singing *I Love a Lassie*. "Have you been singing it in school again?" I asked.

"No, that's just a Valentine's Day one." Whenever we were in the car together she would ask me to play 'the music', except when Granddad was with us, because she knew he didn't like it.

My daughter and a friend were also staying with us for a while, and we went for various outings. I got the usual request from my granddaughter every time, until I thought the others must be getting sick of it (it's not really their kind of music), so I said: -

"I think we should play something different today, just for a change. Is that a good idea?"

Daughter and friend – "Yes!"

Granddaughter – "No!"

"Well I'll tell you what, we'll play something different just now, and play our music on the way home. That's fair enough, isn't it?"

No answer – she knew it was fair but she wasn't happy. She sulked so long that she fell asleep – a five-year-old on the way to the seaside! She didn't forget, either – we had to keep our promise and play it on the way home.

In September of the same year I was visiting her in Aberdeen, and I showed her the tape case with his photograph on the front: -

"That's the man on the tape, singing the songs," I told her.

"He's wearing a red jacket. I thought he wore black clothes. Why is he wearing a red jacket?"

"Because he's wearing a kilt."

"Why?"

"Because he's a Scotsman – Scotsmen like wearing kilts sometimes."

"What's his name?"

"Jimmy Logan."

"He does some *lovely* songs."

This last was said with feeling – the girl had taste. She gets embarrassed when I mention it these days – she's into Gareth Gates and Busted now.

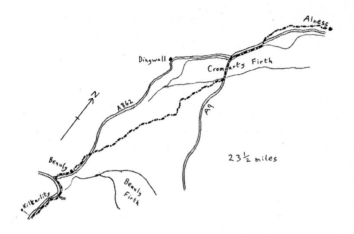

After the usual photo session, they drop me back at the main road, at the same spot where they picked me up yesterday. I'm still not cheating! It's raining today, not heavily but fairly steadily. As I walk up the road towards Beauly, I clear some of the grids with my stick.

It is widely believed that the name of Beauly, from the French *Beau Lieu,* comes from a comment made by Mary Queen of Scots when she visited the priory here in 1564, but it is more likely that the name arose up to three-hundred years earlier, the monks describing it as *Prioratus de Bello Loco*. Nowadays the priory is mostly in ruins.

Just north of the town, Brian and my granddaughter meet me again. They have been doing some sightseeing in the two hours since we parted, and are about to head back to Aberdeen, where Brian will be staying with our son until next weekend.

It's now a long, hard, dreary road, bypassing Muir of Ord, and through Newmore to Easter Kinkell. At Newmore is an unusual monument opposite a school. The rain has eased off a bit, but it's still rather damp. I can just make out through the murkiness, the town of Dingwall, the birthplace of Macbeth, on the other side of the Cromarty Firth. A donkey says hello, and I pass a very pretty church at Ferintosh, with a small tower built on the side for its single bell. There's always something interesting to see, however dismal the road and the weather are.

I reach the A9 and cross the Cromarty Firth bridge, which is over a mile long. In the distance, nearer the mouth of the firth, oil rigs are moored off the port of Invergordon.

The Cromarty Firth is a fine natural harbour – its deep water can easily accommodate the largest cruise liners such as the QE2. The port at Invergordon has traditionally been used for the transportation of natural resources – the area has really come into its own with the development of North Sea oil.

The A9 runs along the shore of the firth. After a while I leave it to follow a quieter road through the village of Evanton. Just north of the village is a fine strip of beech trees beside the road – they will be beautiful in any season.

I'm getting very weary now. It's been a long day, in fact it's been a long seven weeks. Today has been rather depressing, and I still have about three miles to go to Alness. I get there eventually and find my way to the hotel. It's rather drab and basic, but cheap enough, and the staff are friendly. They provide me with a large plateful of plaice and chips, which I tuck into eagerly. I have nearly finished and am contemplating chocolate fudge cake for afters, when I suddenly start to feel faint. I think the problem is that I ate my meal too quickly, after being over-tired, over-hungry, and possibly dehydrated too. I remember that I only stopped briefly for a quick bite at lunchtime, the weather being so wet. I shall have to look after myself better.

The waitress brings me a glass of water and I soon recover – I can't face any pudding though.

Monday 19/4/2004

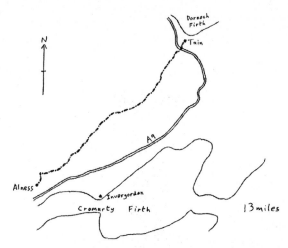

A large breakfast boosts my energy and my spirits. At least I've got a nice short day today. Before I leave Alness I get my form stamped and stock up on food. Then I take the road up past the golf course, and turn onto a good country road which will take me all the way to Tain.

As I amble up this pleasant road, which rises and falls gently, I can look across the firth and see the oil rigs that I mentioned yesterday, closer now, and clearer, now that the weather has improved. An old people's home that I pass is called Newmore House – yes it's the same name as the place with the monument that I passed yesterday, though I didn't realise it until I was writing this book.

I pass a forest where many of the trees are covered in lichen, just as they were near Fort William and have been ever since. Around Scotsburn the scenery is lovely, with a wooded hillside forming a backdrop for a prosperous-looking farm. Lamington village is about two miles long, all strung out thinly along the road.

And so I descend into Tain, Scotland's oldest Royal Burgh, crossing the A9 which bypasses this attractive little town on the

145

edge of the Dornoch Firth.

It is still only mid-afternoon, so I explore the town for a while before looking for my B&B. When I arrive I have plenty of time to relax, have a bath, and cut my toenails (I've had no new blisters since Wolverhampton), before going for a meal. The place my landlady recommends is excellent and I have a fine piece of grilled salmon. Then my daughter phones just as I'm tucking into sticky toffee pudding and custard. Lovely! (The pudding and the phone call).

There is a beautiful sunset as I make my way back to the B&B, so I take some photos.

CHAPTER SIXTEEN

Oh what a beautiful morning
Oh what a beautiful day,
I've got a beautiful feeling,
Everything's going my way

Tuesday 20/4/2004

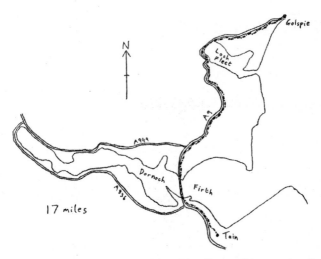

I share my breakfast table with a friendly gentleman who shows an interest in my Walk – he writes me a cheque for ten pounds.

It's a beautiful morning – a clear blue sky with just a few fluffy clouds. The road out of Tain passes a supermarket, where I get some supplies. My phone rings as I walk out across the car park. It's my brother – that's a turn up for the book! He's not normally very communicative so it's nice to know he's thinking about me.

I reach the bypass, and now it will be the A9 all the way today as there's not much choice of route here. Just outside the town is the Glen Morangie distillery. Then I'm onto the Dornoch Firth bridge, which was built in the 1980s, saving nearly twenty miles.

The sun continues to shine as I march up this fine road through scattered communities such as Clashmore and Evelix. The population of the North of Scotland is very thinly spread. I get more phone calls – Tom at work phones to check on my progress, then the lady at Lybster, where I'm booked for the day after tomorrow, phones to say that she's double-booked and can't accommodate me. But it's alright as she's arranged a bed for me at her friend's house down the road.

There aren't many cars about, but some of those that are, greet me with a beep and a wave – or rather their occupants do. I suppose anyone who is mad enough to be walking up the A9 with a rucksack and stick must be an End-to-Ender. It's a great feeling, especially when I think that I've nearly reached my goal – only four days after today.

I see a dead chaffinch beside the road, and it makes me think of the old Marianne Faithful song 'This little bird, that somebody sent'. The song is running through my head now. Later I pass a dead deer lying in a ditch – I suppose it must have been hit by a vehicle.

The road comes to The Mound, a causeway built in 1816 by Thomas Telford (again!), separating Strath Fleet from Loch Fleet, a sea loch whose entrance is a narrow channel with strong tidal currents. Large sluice gates let migrating salmon through the causeway, and the loch is a National Nature Reserve – a haven for many different kinds of wildlife and a birdwatcher's paradise.

Just a few miles further and I am in Golspie, the statue of the Duke of Sutherland standing guard on his hilltop above the town. This man was responsible for evicting thousands of tenants to make way for sheep in the early nineteenth century, as part of the Highland Clearances.

The sky has been gradually clouding over since midday, and there is a shower of rain as I arrive at my B&B, a fine granite house in a side street. I am given a warm welcome by Alan and Jane, who only took over the business three weeks ago. In fact Alan only took up permanent residence today, having been 'commuting' from Derby. He says he passed me on the road today, on his motorbike. When they hear that I am walking for charity, they upgrade my room from a single to a double with en suite shower room.

They invite me to share a sausage casserole (I'm their only guest tonight), and ask my opinion as to what constitutes a good B&B. The house has been decorated and furnished in a very bland, modern style, and I agree that it would be much nicer in a more traditional style, in keeping with the age and type of the building. They can't decide whether to have a television in the residents' lounge (in addition to the bedrooms), as it would tend to kill conversation – I suggest they could compromise with a small, unobtrusive one.

Before re-inventing herself as a B&B landlady, Jane was an IT (information technology) manager at Rolls Royce in Derby. There she liaised with people from the IT company EDS, who have a contract there. This is the same company that I work for in Telford. Small world! Also her father used to be Chief Engineer for the Dundee Area of the North of Scotland Hydro-Electric Board, that I used to work for when we lived near Aberdeen.

For twenty-two years, Alan worked for Mars, the confectionery company. He says that Mr Mars was a lovely man with no snobbishness, the sort of man who would happily queue at a coffee machine with his employees, and have a conversation with them.

Wednesday 21/4/2004

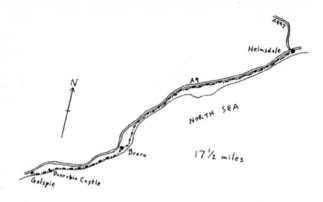

Before I leave, we discuss today's route. My map shows a path along the shore, but I'm not sure of its status. Jane and Alan haven't been here long enough to know it themselves, but they manage to dig out a tourist leaflet which gives details of it, so that's okay.

I take my leave and go to the newsagent for some snacks. "Are you going up or down?" asks the shopkeeper when he sees the sign on my rucksack. I also visit the Post Office, then find my way to the coastal footpath by way of a footbridge over a burn (there's a ford for vehicles) and a gate into a large meadow beside the shore.

A strong, cold wind is against me as I follow the path, but at least it's dry. The path passes in front of Dunrobin Castle, a fairytale castle which has long been home to the Dukes and Earls of Sutherland. With 189 rooms, it is the largest home in Northern Scotland, and is one of Britain's oldest continuously inhabited houses, partially dating from the early fourteenth century.

The path continues through a wood, then on to more meadowland. At the top of the field is a broch – this is the remains of an Iron Age fortified dwelling. Further along, the path drops down beside the Sputie Burn waterfall, which emerges directly onto the beach. I find out later that this is a good spot for seal watching, but there are none about today.

150

Perhaps it's the wrong time of year, or maybe I'm just not very observant.

Eventually I reach Brora, where I have to go up to the main road in order to cross the river Brora. The clock in its fine stone tower tells me that the time is twenty-five past eight – I don't think that's right! The map shows the coastal footpath continuing round the golf course for a couple of miles, though it's not included on the tourist leaflet from Golspie. I think I'll risk it as it will be better than the road, and I won't have much choice later. It is most enjoyable, and I stop for lunch half way. Unfortunately the path peters out at the top end, and I have some difficulty finding the way across the railway onto the road. At last I find a stile, not a very good one, which takes me on to the railway track. There is no bridge so I have to look out for trains, then climb a fence the other side. Now just a field with a gate separates me from the road.

It's the A9 all the way to Helmsdale now, past the scattered communities of Lothbeg and Lothmore. I eat an apple as I walk along, but am interrupted by the phone. It is a reporter from the *Mearns Leader*, the local weekly paper in Stonehaven. Brian has called in to the office to try and get some publicity for me, as we know a lot of people in the Stonehaven area. The reporter asks me lots of questions that I am happy to answer, and I describe how walking has become a way of life – "It's what I do now." (Not for much longer though.)

And so I drop down through Portgower to the small town of Helmsdale, with its harbour, Tourist Centre, and modern bridge over the river. My landlady has given me directions and I soon find the house – there are ducks in the garden. On greeting me, she asks if I would prefer hen eggs or duck eggs for breakfast. I have to explain that, much as I love duck eggs, unfortunately they don't like me. I found this out years ago, when we used to keep poultry ourselves – they made me very ill, very quickly!

She brings me a glass of milk and some cheese and biscuits, and recommends an award winning fish-and-chip restaurant in the town. I follow her advice and find it excellent. There was no signal on the mobile in the house so I wander about a bit, and finally get a signal on the old bridge.

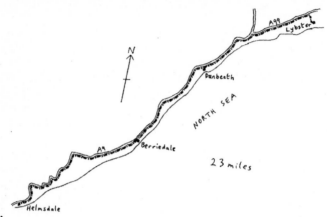

Last night, the landlady asked me what time I would like breakfast today, so I asked for seven o'clock as I've got a long day today. She puts a huge plateful of sausages, bacon, eggs, mushrooms, etc in front of me – "I'll never eat all that," I protest. I do manage it though. She gets quite talkative, asking lots of questions about my Walk – she wants to know how I manage for toilets.

It is eight-thirty by the time I leave. Another beautiful morning. Brian phones to see how I'm getting on – I've only done about a mile, just climbing the hill out of the town. I'm still on the A9; there's no choice today.

Once the road has risen away from the rocky coast, it follows the contours round a number of hairpin bends, where burns form deep ravines in the steep hillside. Some of the bends are not as sharp as they used to be; the road has been upgraded and the redundant section of road with its old bridge over the burn can be seen alongside the new bridge.

At the Sutherland/Caithness border is a car park with a viewpoint. I can see right across to Tain, where I was two days ago. At the edge of the car park a small stone plaque bears the inscription "Wm Welch perished here 31st Jany 1878 Be ye also ready". I wonder who he was, and how he died?

I am approaching Berriedale, where the notorious braes on the north side are reputed to be a tough climb. Roadworks are in place, starting a mile before the village, with one-way traffic controlled by traffic lights. I wouldn't like to be in a car here just now – it looks as though it's one-way right down to the village. Halfway down, I see a man with a large rucksack coming the other way. We greet each other and discover that we both have the same goal, or rather precisely opposite goals. His name is Ian and he set out from John O'Groats two days ago. We sit on the crash barrier and discuss tactics – he is camping every night. I couldn't do that, but then he is quite a bit younger than me. We wish each other luck and go our separate ways.

Having reached Berriedale village, I go into a cafe for some light lunch. The cafe also sells bric-a-brac, and I can't resist looking around, even though there's no point in buying anything as I couldn't possibly carry it. Now I have to tackle the Braes of Berriedale, a steep hill with sharp zigzags. Everyone said I would find it hard, but I am surprised how easily I get to the top. I must be fit. Of course any road, however steep, is never as difficult as a mountain path such as Jacob's Ladder on Kinder Scout, or the Devil's Staircase on the West Highland Way.

As I continue up the road, I get my weekly phone call from Mike – it's only Thursday but he's on holiday tomorrow. He's pleased to hear that I'm on target to finish on Saturday.

At Borgue a nice old man comes out of his driveway and crosses the road to talk to me. He says he hasn't been to John O'Groats for years, but used to go there often for motorbike rallies.

Approaching Dunbeath I have a good view of the castle perched on the cliffs. It is still lived in but is not open to the public. It looks well-maintained with its cream walls.

Brian phones again, just as I'm crossing the fine modern bridge over the river, built in 1989 to replace the old one built about 1815 by Thomas Telford. (That man got about a bit!) Brian used to drive a lorry in this part of the world, delivering steel from Aberdeen, and the road used to be more difficult, zigzagging back on itself to negotiate the old bridge.

Just beyond Dunbeath I come across the Laidhay Croft

Museum, which isn't marked on my map. I remember it though as we visited it a long time ago – it must be at least twenty years – on the only previous occasion that we ventured as far as John O'Groats. I don't think it had a tearoom then. It's an interesting museum, showing how life was lived way back then, but I don't bother with it today; I just visit the tearoom for a snack and to use the facilities.

Refreshed, I carry on through Latheronwheel and Latheron, where the road splits, the A9 heading north to Thurso, and the A99 continuing close to the coast to eventually reach John O'Groats. I shall be taking a different route tomorrow though.

There are small wild flowers beside the road in this area. I think the purple ones may be thyme, but I don't recognise the white flowers of a similar size. About two miles before Lybster, my phone rings again. It's my mother, checking whether I'm on target. I think I've finally convinced her that I'm actually going to manage it.

Lybster consists of a long, wide main street, with grey stone houses both sides, stretching for nearly a mile between road and coast. I'm not sure how far down my B&B is – I hope it's not too far as it's been a long day today. Of course it's nearly at the bottom, and on the way I pass the place where I was supposed to be staying, before it was double-booked. While I'm looking for it, a young girl, about eleven years old, passes me on a scooter – "Would you like a go?" she asks. "No thank you," I reply with a smile.

I am glad to relax and have a bath when I arrive. I still have a pot noodle in my rucksack; it has been there a while now. I might as well use it, it will save going out again, though I think it will be a long time before I ever have another one. I send my daughter a text and she phones for a chat. Later I go down to the sitting room for a pleasant conversation with the friendly landlady.

CHAPTER SEVENTEEN

Keep right on to
the end of the road
Keep right on to the end

Friday 23/4/2004

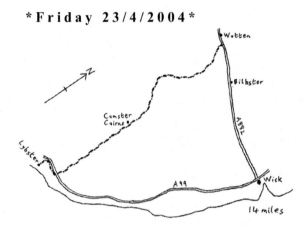

Before I leave, the landlady makes me some cheese sandwiches for a packed lunch. On the way out of the village, I call at the Post Office to get my form stamped for the last time before the end, and to buy stamps for the many postcards I'll have to write when I've finished.

Then I cross the road to a proper old-fashioned grocery shop, which has been in the same family since 1890. It's not self-service, you have to ask for what you want, just like when I was a child. He hasn't got a modern till – he adds up my purchases by hand. His wife (whose family home was the house where I stayed last night) goes through to the house behind the shop, and comes back with a bag of home-made shortbread for me.

The bank doesn't have a cash machine, I have to go inside

to get some money. I'm quite sorry to leave Lybster – it's not a particularly pretty village, but it certainly has its charms.

A mile beyond the village, I leave the main road, turning left up a country road towards Watten, thus bypassing Wick. The distance is probably about the same, and I'll have some peace from the traffic at last (not that there's very much of it here). Near the junction I see a sign for a cheese factory a bit further up the main road. It's tempting. I love cheese, but I don't really want any diversions, and it would be more to carry. Perhaps we can call in when we're driving back down on Sunday.

I pass a house called 'Station House'. It is on the course of a dismantled railway line, the former Wick and Lybster light railway that opened in 1903 and closed in 1944. Lybster Golf Club now uses the old ticket office as a clubhouse.

This road is long and straight for miles, with isolated farms along the way. About noon I reach the Grey Cairns of Camster. These are very impressive Iron Age chambered cairns, well worth a visit – I imagine most tourists miss them, as they are off the beaten track, though they are signposted from the main road. They are very well looked after, with wooden walkways built across the bog to reach them.

Just as I'm investigating them more closely, Brian arrives in the car. The entrances to the cairns have little iron gates, so he tells me to get inside so that he can take a photo of me behind bars. There is a passage that goes right inside to the chamber, but you have to crawl, and I don't fancy it – I don't suppose there's much to see anyway.

After more photos and filming, we sit in the car to eat lunch. Then he drives away, leaving me to walk on through the rain which has been threatening all day.

This is Flow country – vast square miles of peat bog, some of which is covered with large conifer plantations. I pass places where the peat has recently been cut for fuel. The road here is unfenced and half-a-dozen sheep are wandering down it.

A cyclist is coming down the road towards me – he doesn't look very confident as he's wavering all over the road. He's a middle-aged gentleman on his way to Land's End in aid of Cancer Research, planning to go via Newcastle because he lives there. I guess he hasn't got used to carrying his luggage on the bike – I hope he makes it safely.

Eventually I come close to Watten. Here the land is more cultivated and some of the fields are separated by fences made from slabs of Caithness slate. At the junction close to the village, Brian picks me up and drives me two miles down the road to our B&B at Bilbster. It is a lovely old house that they are running as a business so they can afford to keep living in it. The landlord brings us tea and biscuits, and introduces us to his three-year-old twin boys, who want to show us their umbrellas.

Our room is enormous, full of beautiful walnut furniture. The en suite bathroom is also huge – Brian has a shower while I soak in a bath that takes a criminal amount of hot water to fill.

Later we drive to Watten for a meal. We go the long way round to have a look at the surrounding countryside. This involves driving over a level crossing on the Thurso to Wick line, where I have to use the telephone to check that there are no trains due. Further on we see a deer running across the moss, and stop to watch it.

As we settle down for the night in the lovely old bed, with traditional blankets rather than a duvet, I have mixed emotions. Tomorrow is my last day, and I don't know whether to be happy or sad, relieved or excited.

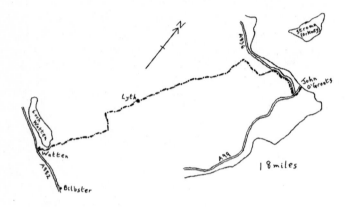

Though the way be long, let your heart be strong,
Keep right on round the bend

Am I round the bend? No, I don't think so. In fact I think I'm saner than I've ever been in my life.

Brian drops me off at the junction where he picked me up yesterday, and I start my last day's walk with the half a mile of road into Watten village. Watten is the birthplace of Alexander Bain. (What do you mean, you've never heard of him?) He invented an electric clock, and was the first person to use the telegraph to transmit time signals, thus standardising time throughout Britain, of great benefit to the railway system. He also patented a telegraphic fax machine, thirty years before the telephone was invented.

For the past couple of days, my legs have been getting weary. It's as if they know that the end is in sight. They keep saying to me 'Can't we stop yet?' and I reply 'Keep going, we're nearly there, you can stop soon'. Yes, I'm talking to my legs now. Perhaps I am round the bend after all.

I pass Watten Loch, a pretty loch loved by trout fishers. Further on, at Quoybrae, is a venue for a regular livestock mart.

Later, at Hastigrow, on a road which joins Wick and Thurso, I see another deer.

From here the road is dead straight for miles again, rising and falling gently. It is very pleasant walking, with virtually no traffic. At Lyth is a War Memorial at the crossroads, and an Arts Centre which unfortunately is half a mile in the wrong direction. It's probably closed anyway, and I'm not in the mood for diversions – I just want to get to my destination.

Brian catches up with me just north of Lyth – it's a good job I didn't go to the Arts Centre, he wouldn't have been able to find me. He asks me where I'll be by lunchtime, and we arrange to meet up near Slickly, about three miles up the road. When I reach the small group of houses and a farm, there is no sign of him. My phone rings. "Where are you?" he says. "I'm at Slickly, where are you?" He says he's just up the road, waiting for me. The road rises slightly to the brow of a hill, so it's not until I reach the top that I spot the car in the distance – about a mile further on! Eventually I get there and we sit in the car to eat lunch together.

Then he zooms off, driving round to kill time while I continue my journey. I approach the brow of another hill, where a transmitter stands beside the road. As I come over the top, a whole new vista greets me. At last I can see the northern coast, two miles away, and the Orkney Islands beyond. It's an exhilarating moment.

I drop down to Upper Gills, where an old lady is digging the verge in front of her house, in preparation for planting flowers. I tell her about my Walk and she asks me if anyone is meeting me at John O'Groats. "Oh yes, I've seen the blue car going up and down the road," she says, when I explain about Brian. She invites me in for a cup of tea, but I'm anxious to get on.

There's only a few miles to go now. Part of me wants to get there as quickly as possible, part doesn't want it all to end.

The road takes me through the village of Canisbay. There is a Youth Hostel here, where the gentleman cyclist I met yesterday stayed before he started his journey. Then I'm down onto the main coast road from Thurso. Soon I can see the old

John O'Groats Hotel across the fields. The road goes first to the village, meeting the road from Wick.

As I turn the last corner, it starts to rain. Typical! The End is in sight, and it's not worth donning the waterproofs for this short distance. Brian meets me at the entrance to the car park, camcorder in hand, and he films me as I make my way to the signpost. I did it!

Next we go into the bar of the hotel (which no longer functions as a hotel, and is looking rather run down), where I sign the book of End-to-Enders, and celebrate with a pint of cider. I don't normally drink much, so I really should have asked for a half. I enjoy it, but it goes straight to my head, and Brian films me staggering across the car park.

My Journey is over. I am left with a deep sense of satisfaction, although there's still a feeling of unreality about it. Did I really walk 972 miles in eight weeks, or was it all a figment of my imagination?

Though you're tired and weary, still journey on,
Till you come to your happy abode,
Where all you love and you're dreaming of
Will be there, at the end of the road.

CHAPTER EIGHTEEN

Back to life
Back to reality

The next day we drove to Aberdeen to stay with our son (and yes, we did visit the cheese factory on the way). I drove for about fifty miles, which felt very odd, but then my knees seized up and became quite painful. They actually ached for the next six weeks – they were telling me that they needed to rest for a while.

After spending a couple of days visiting friends in the area, we came back home to Wales. As we drove into Adfa, we noticed some balloons tied to a post. "It must be someone's birthday," I said. Then we saw the signs – 'Welcome home Kath', 'Congratulations' – they were all over the village and at the end of our track; even some on our house, with more balloons. I was thrilled that the villagers were so supportive, especially with the Bingo Night – we've only lived here five years and it can sometimes take a lot longer to be accepted in a rural community.

The following week I returned to work – back to reality. But what is reality? It's something I was searching for on the Walk – and am still searching for. Sitting in front of a computer screen all day certainly isn't reality, though it does pay the mortgage.

Maybe reality isn't something you search *for*, maybe it's the search itself. If I can quote from *Zen and the Art of Motorcycle Maintenance*:-

"You look at where you're going and where you are, and it never makes sense, but then you look back at where you've been and a pattern seems to emerge. And if you project forward from that pattern, then sometimes you can come up with something."

That's certainly the way it seems to have worked for me – various events in my life led up to me doing the Walk, as I have tried to explain in the chapters of this book. I'm still not sure where I go from here though.

I sometimes feel I would like to go back in time, experience the whole thing all over again – perhaps I could capture the reality that eluded me the first time. I was too obsessed with the practicalities of the journey, constantly checking the map and working out how much further I had to go that day, and what time I was likely to arrive.

Somehow I didn't seem to have time to have deep philosophical discussions with myself, but at least it was a great escape from the complexities of modern life. In a way I envy tramps. Theirs must be a great hassle-free lifestyle, except for sleeping in barns and such like – I don't think I'd fancy that.

I can't honestly say I have found the meaning of life, though I am certainly more contented and have a better understanding of what is important and what isn't.

But why should life have to have a meaning anyway? Life just *is*. So make of it what you will. Enjoy it. *Do* something. If you can leave your mark on the world, in a constructive way, then maybe that is meaning enough.

Well that's enough rambling. I'm not sure what it all means, but hopefully it's given you some food for thought…